Mair EDINBUGGERS

VS.
Merr WEEGIES

**Mair 'friendly' rivalry
and anti-Weegie swedging**

EDINBUGGERS START HERE

First published 2005
by Black & White Publishing Ltd
29 Ocean Drive, Edinburgh EH6 6JL

Reprinted 2005, 2008

ISBN 978 1 84502 072 9

Text © Ian Black 2005
Cover illustration © Bob Dewar 2005

British Library Cataloguing in Publication Data:
A catalogue record for this book is available
from the British Library.

Cover illustration by Bob Dewar

Printed and bound by Norhaven A/S

INTRODUCTION

Every Edinbugger worth his or her salt and sauce knows that talk is cheap in Glasgow because supply exceeds demand and that the first question at a Glasgow pub quiz is, 'What are you looking at?' – but not many know why the River Clyde runs through Glasgow. The answer being, of course, that if it walked it would get mugged.

Tens of thousands of Edinbuggers seeking answers to questions like the above were generous enough to buy copies of *Edinbuggers vs Weegies*, the last collection of Weegie-baiting scribblings. Nearly as many bought it in the capital as did in Glasgow, a surprising statistic given the disparity in populations and possibly bearing out the Edinbugger assertions regarding the literacy levels of the Weegies.

It has been asserted that Weegies are so dense that light bends around them and if you stand close enough to one – not that one would want to, but if you do – you can hear the sea.

The effusive over-friendliness of your oh-so-very-average Weegie is dealt with in these pages, as is the instant aggression at any questioning that they are right every time, even about sectarianism, a blight that persists still like some malign and replicating cancer at all levels of Glasgow society. You will read of neds and chavs, the latter being Edinburgh's pale copy of the full-blown Weegie headcase, and you may learn that parents from Possil in Glasgow are incredibly hard, but they never smack their children. Well, maybe one or two grams to get them to sleep at night.

Here is a further collection of jibes and diatribes about the tribe known as the Weegies. Some are true. Some are not. The challenge is to tell them apart.

But it is just friendly jesting. Sure it is. Not.

1
ATTITUDES AND INSULTS

Weegie Compliments

Hur, she could shoplift in a kebab shoap.

At the conclusion of a more than satisfactory repast
– 'I've et worse.'

You want to feel really handsome, svelte and successful? Go shopping at Tesco in Glasgow.

There's many a Glasgow man with the heart of a little child. They usually keep them in jars.

What's the difference between a Weegie and a sperm?
   A sperm has one chance in ten million of becoming a human being.

How many Weegies does it take to change a light bulb?
   It doesn't matter, they're all condemned to eternal darkness anyway.

What do you get when you cross a Weegie with a pig?

I don't know, there are some things a pig just won't do.

What's the difference between a wedding and a wake in Glasgow?

There's one less drunk at a wake.

Q. Why wasn't Jesus born in Glasgow?
A. Because God couldn't find three wise men and a virgin.

Why are they putting Weegies at the bottom of the sea?

They found out that deep down, they're really not so bad.

Why has Edinburgh got AIDS and Glasgow has Celtic and Rangers?

Because Edinburgh had first choice.

Two Weegies jump off a cliff, which one hits the ground first?

Who gives a fuck?

Weegies got into the gene pool when the lifeguard wasn't looking.

One-celled organisms outscore them in IQ tests.

Prime candidates for natural deselection.

As bright as Possil in December.

Weegies are so dense that light bends around them.

If you stand close enough to a Weegie, you can hear the sea.

Parents from Possil in Glasgow are incredibly hard, but they never smack their children.

Well, maybe one or two grams to get them to sleep at night.

2

THE JOY OF SECTARIANISM

One of the joys of living in Glasgow is football sectarian humour, an endless source of jolly fun for all concerned, and almost always completely inter-changeable, as in, 'I'd rather be Bin Laden than a Tim.' Change the word Tim to Hun and voila! Here is a song that could easily be changed around. And I know someone will.

Dedicated Follower of Rangers
Tune: 'Dedicated Follower of Fashion'

His teeth are green, his head is square,
Wi' a big moustache, and curly hair.
One day he's on Paisley Road, the next day he's in jail.
He's a dedicated follower of Rangers.

He hates the Tims, he loves the Queen
A naked burd, he's never seen.
He holidays in Airdrie and his breath would
make ye scream.
He's a dedicated follower of Rangers.

He likes to sing: 'Hello, Hello.'
He likes to drink . . . El Dor-a-do.
There's one thing that he hates and that is cleanliness.
He thinks that Derek Johnstone is a handsome,
                                        witty man.
He's a dedicated follower of Rangers.

His team get gubbed in a foreign land,
And once again, he's on remand,
But he knows a real good lawyer from his local
                                        marching band.
He's a dedicated follower of Rangers.

He bangs the drum . . . in Motherwell.
He bares the bum . . . ootside chap-el.
He'd probably be a champ if being a fanny was a sport.
He's a dedicated follower of Rangers.

What's 400 metres long and has an arsehole every 2 feet?

The Orange Walk.

Donald Findlay QC, a Hun who does most of his best work in Edinburgh, has not had his troubles to seek and has obviously not heard the saying, 'A closed mouth gathers no feet.'

Speaking in Larne, Northern Ireland, Donald asked an audience of Rangers supporters: 'It's very smoky in here tonight – has another fucking Pope died?' an unusual sectarian joke in that it is non-reversible. And funny.

But the world has fallen on his head and I fear that we will no longer have the opportunity to hear even his court stories, one of which concerns one of his clients being questioned by the Strathclyde polis. 'Where were you between seven and eleven?' growled the copper.

Donald's client cracked back: 'Primary school. Where were you?'

Traffic was backed up for miles on the M8 in the East End of Glasgow, and the police were going from car to car. When they got to my car I asked the polis what was going on.

He said, 'It's Donald Findlay, QC. He's up there threatening to set himself on fire. Says he's being persecuted for his beliefs. We are going from car to car collecting donations.'

'Donations?' I said, 'How much have you got so far?'

He said, 'About ten gallons.'

A Hun, a Muslim and a Hindu are travelling together on a journey. Night comes and they arrive at a hotel to find that there are only two beds available and that one of them will have to sleep in the barn outside.

The Muslim agrees to sleep in the barn. However, he returns two minutes later and states that he cannot sleep in the barn because there is a pig in it. The Hindu agrees to swap places with him and heads off to the barn. But it isn't long before he too returns, stating that he cannot sleep in the barn because there is a cow in there. Reluctantly, the Hun agrees to sleep in the barn instead. Two minutes later the pig and the cow turn up at the room.

3
DEAD WEEGIES

Why aren't there more?

When Big Peter Reid dies in Glasgow, his old widow wishes to tell all his friends at once, so she goes to the newspaper and says, 'I'd like tae place an obituary fur ma late husband.' The man at the desk says, 'OK, how much money huv ye got?' The old woman replies, '£5,' to which the man says, 'You won't get many words for that but write something and we'll see if it's OK.' So the old woman writes something and hands it over the counter. The man reads, 'Peter Reid, fae Parkheid: deid.' The advertising clerk feels guilty at the abrupt-ness of the statement and encourages her to add something else. The old woman ponders and then adds a few more words and hands the paper over the counter again. The clerk then reads, 'Peter Reid, fae Parkheid: deid. Vauxhall Nova for sale.'

4
MENTAL WELLNESS

NHS cutbacks are going a bit far. This is, allegedly, the message you receive when you phone a well-known Glasgow hospital:

'Hello, you have reached the Psychiatric Clinic.
If you are obsessive-compulsive, press 1 repeatedly.
If you are co-dependent, have someone press 2 for you.
If you are paranoid, we know who you are. Stay on the line so we can trace this call.
If you suffer from multiple personality disorder, press 3, 4 and 5.
If you are suffering from a schizophrenic personality disorder, wait for a little voice to tell you which number to press.
If you are paranoid-delusional, we know who you are and what you want. Just stay on the line so we can trace the call.
If you are depressed, it doesn't matter which number you press. No one will answer. Ever.
If you are delusional and occasionally hallucinate,

please be aware that the thing you are holding to the side of your head is alive and about to bite your ear off.'

The psychology instructor at Heriot Watt had just finished a lecture on mental health and was giving an oral test.

'What would you call a patient who walks back and forth screaming at the top of his lungs one minute, then sits in a chair weeping uncontrollably the next?'

An Edinbugger at the back raised his hand and asked, 'The Rangers manager?'

5
ANOTHER WORD TO THE WISE

This is a real sign in a Glasgow shop:

'Warning to shoplifters: Anyone caught shoplifting will be gagged, beaten, whipped and tortured. Any survivors will be prosecuted to the full extent of the law.'

6

WEEGIE LORD'S PRAYER

Our Lager,
Which art in barrels,
Hallowed be thy drink.
Thy will be drunk, (I will be drunk)
At home, as it is in the pub.
Give us this day our foamy head.
And forgive us our spillages,
As we forgive those who spill against us.
And lead us not to incarceration,
But deliver us from hangovers.
For thine is the beer, the heavy and the lager.
For ever and ever.
Barmen

7
JENNERS IS AN INSTITUTION

A young Weegie is hired by Jenners and reports for his first day of work.

The manager greets him with a hearty handshake and smile, hands him a brush and says, 'Your first job will be to sweep out the store.'

'Sweep the store, but I'm a graduate of Caledonian University,' the young man indignantly replied.

'Oh, I'm sorry. I didn't know that,' said the manager. 'Here, give me the brush – I'll show you how.'

A keen Weegie lad applied for a salesman's job in Jenners back in the days when you could buy just about anything there. The supervisor asked him, 'Have you ever been a salesman before?'

He replied confidently that he had. The guy liked the cut of his jib and said, 'You can start tomorrow and I'll come and see you when we close up.'

The day was long and arduous for the young man, but finally 5 o'clock came around. The supervisor duly turned up and asked: 'How many sales did you make today?'

'One,' said the Weegie.

'Only one?' he said. 'Most of the staff make 20 or 30 sales a day. How much was the sale worth?'

'Three hundred thousand pounds,' said the young man with a cheeky Weegie grin.

'How did you manage that?' asked the flabbergasted boss.

'Well,' said the salesman, 'this guy came in and I sold him a wee fish hook, then a medium hook and finally a really big hook. Then I sold him a small fishing line, a medium one and a huge big one. I asked him where he was going fishing and he said down the coast.

I said he would probably need a boat, so I took him down to the boat department and sold him that twenty footer with the twin engines. Then he said his Volkswagen probably wouldn't be able to pull it, so I took him to the car department and sold him a great big 4-wheeler.'

The supervisor took two steps back and asked in astonishment, 'You sold all that to a guy who came in for a fish hook?'

'Naw,' answered the Weegie. 'He came in to buy a box of Tampax for his wife and I said to him, 'Your weekend's knackered, pal. You might as well go fishing.'

8
TRUE STORY

A Weegie school teacher injured his back over the summer holidays and had to wear a plaster cast around the upper part of his body. It fitted neatly under his shirt and was not noticeable at all.

On the first day at his new school in Craigmillar, still with the cast under his shirt, he found himself assigned to the worst behaved class in the school.

He walked into the rowdy classroom, opened the window as wide as possible and then busied himself with desk work. When a strong breeze made his tie flap, he took the stapler from his desk and stapled the tie to his chest. Oddly, he had no trouble with discipline that year, and for the next few years he was known as The Iron Weegie.

9
THE WEALTH OF NATIONS

Late one night in Holyrood, a chav wearing a ski mask jumped into the path of a well-dressed man and flashed a stakey* at him.

'Give me your money!' he demanded.

Indignant, the well-dressed man bellowed, 'Do you realize that you are attempting to rob an MSP?'

'Is that a fact?' replied the robber. 'Then give me ma money!'

*See Neducation section.

10
ARSEHOLE, LOOPHOLE

What's the definition of a good Edinburgh accountant? Someone who has a loophole named after him.

11
A WUNCH OF BANKERS

A torn-arsed Weegie in trackies walks into an Edinburgh bank and says to the female teller, 'I want to open a fuckin' account.' To which the woman replied, 'I beg your pardon, what did you say?'

'Listen deefie, I said I want to open a fuckin' account right now.'

'I'm sorry sir, but we do not tolerate that kind of language in this bank,' she replied. Then the woman left her desk and went through to the bank manager and told him about her situation. They both returned and the manager asked, 'What seems to be the problem here?'

'There's no bastard problem,' the man said, 'I just won 16 million quid in the lottery and I want to open a fuckin' account at this fuckin' bank!'

'I see, sir,' the manager said, 'and is this fucking bitch giving you grief?'

12
HOUSEY HOUSEY

Q. How do you get four old ladies in Corstorphine to swear?
A. Get the fifth old woman to shout, 'Bingo!'

19
THE LORD GOD AND EDINBUGGERS

Standing on the Portobello shore, an Edinbugger lady watches her grandson playing with the jobbies in the water. She is thunderstruck when she sees a huge wave crash over him. When it recedes, the boy is no longer there. He has vanished.

Screaming, the woman holds her hands to the sky and cries, 'Lord, how could you? Have I not been a wonderful mother and grandmother? Have I not scrimped and saved so I could give to the church? Have I not always put others before myself? Have I not always turned my other cheek and loved my neighbours? Have I not –'

A deep, loud Weegie voice from the sky interrupts. 'Moan, moan, moan, moan. Geez a brek, here!'

Immediately, another huge wave appears and crashes on the beach. And when it recedes, the boy is there smiling, splashing around as if nothing ever happened.

The deep loud voice continues, 'Therr's yer boay back. Ur ye happy noo?'

The Edinbugger lady responded, 'He had a hat.'

13
PLUS ÇA CHANGE

A returned Glasgow exile gets in a taxi at the airport and asks to be taken into town. He falls into conversation, as you do, with the taxi driver, and winds up claiming that even after 20 years away he can still recognise Glasgow districts by their smell and by how the air feels.

The driver takes up the challenge and produces a blindfold. (As they do, if asked.) They reach the first district and the guy opens the window, sticks his hand out, finger and thumb rubbing the air, takes a deep breath and says, 'Bearsden.' He is, of course, right and the taxi driver asks, 'How do you do that?' The guy says, 'Oh, I can feel that edge of capitalist competition, that 'I must keep up with the Joneses,' bigger car, better house. Not too pleasant. Bit like Edinburgh.'

The driver then takes him to another district and the guy goes through the same procedure, sticking his arm out etc and says, 'Springburn,' and then explains, 'I can feel all of the nationalities that came here seeking refuge from torture, imprisonment and death in their former countries, their aspirations for their children, the hope that they will be accepted as new Glaswegians. I wish them well.'

The driver is impressed and decides on one final test for the passenger. They get there and one second after he has stuck his hand out and before he has even taken a breath, he says, 'Possil.'

The driver says, 'Jees, that was quick. How can you possibly know?'

The guy says, 'My watch is away.'

Edinbuggers who wish to convert this story to their native city have a wide choice of final district, like Muirhouse, Granton, Niddry, Craigmillar, Wester Hailes, Sighthill, etc. You know where the etc are.

14
IT'S A SIGN

Sign on the roadside near a Glasgow hospital:
Hospital Quiet Zone –
Please Use Silencers On Your Shooters

Sticker on a Glasgow car
Toot if you love peace and quiet

Another sticker on a schemie car
Pardon my driving
I am reloading

15
WEEGIES DO GRASS

One afternoon a wealthy Edinbugger lawyer was driving home from a hard day robbing Weegies when he saw two men along the roadside at Easterhouse eating grass. Curious, he stopped and got out to investigate.

'Why are you eating grass?' he asked one man.

'We don't have any money for food,' said the guy, 'so we have to eat grass.'

'Well then, you can come with me to my house and I'll feed you,' the Edinbugger said.

'But I have a wife and two children. They're over there underneath that tree,' said the guy pathetically.

'That's fine,' replies the lawyer. 'Bring them along too.'

Turning to the other poor sowl he stated, 'You can come with us too.' The second man, in a pitiful voice, said, 'But I have a wife and SIX children with me, some of them mine.'

'Don't worry about it,' the lawyer replies casually. 'You can bring them along as well.'

They all entered the car, which was no easy task,

as even the vast 4x4 nearly wasn't quite big enough. Once underway, one of the poor guys turned to the lawyer and said, 'You are very kind, new friend. Thank you for taking all of us with you.'

The Edinbugger replied, 'Glad to do it. You'll love my place. The grass is nearly a foot high!'

16
SAINTS ALIVE

A wee drunk is walking up the road in Springburn in Glasgow when he sees a bloke jump off a high rise. He blinks and looks up again to see this chap hurtle down, and three feet from the ground, calmly stop and float down gently with no injury!

He blinks like mad and decides there is no way he could have seen that. And then – down comes another! He's now thinking of never touching any alcoholic beverage ever again, but thinks, 'I'm away up that building to see what the fuck is going on!'

So up he goes to the fifteenth floor and out onto the roof where he sees the two guys discussing whether to go again.

'Whit's a' this?' asks he.

'What do you mean, what's all this?' asks one of the men.

'I've just watched youse two jump off the building, hurtle to the floor, then float the last three feet and not a scratch on either of youse! What's going on?'

'Oh that,' says the first guy. 'That's nothing, anyone can do it. They only need confidence that they'll stop.'

'You mean I could do that?'

'No bother at all, ma mannie.'

'Nah, yer joking!'

'No we're not, you saw me doing it, so why not you?'

The wee man thinks for a minute and decides to go for it. He moves to the very edge, looks at the two guys, who say nothing, and jumps. Straight into the ground. Splat! Deid! Not breathing. Separated from his life. Buckfast will be forced into liquidation.

The first of the two blokes turns and says, 'Giles, for a Saint, you can be a right Edinburgh bastard at times!'

17

DEAD SAINTS

St Giles, incidentally, picked the right place to be saint of. As well as looking after Edinburgh, he is saint of beggars, blacksmiths, breast cancer, breast feeding, cancer patients, cripples, disabled people, epilepsy, epileptics, fear of night, forests, handicapped people, hermits, horses, insanity, lepers, leprosy, mental illness, mentally ill people, paupers, poor people, rams, spur makers, and sterility.

He obviously went to the right place, and is he ever busy.

It was not always thus. He was born a wealthy noble. When his parents died, he used his fortune to help the poor. He was a miracle worker, and we are not talking cheapskate here. To avoid followers and adulation, he left Greece c.683AD for France where he lived as a hermit in a cave in the diocese of Nimes, a cave whose mouth was guarded by a thick thorn bush, and a lifestyle so impoverished that, legend says, God sent a hind to him to nourish him with her milk.

One day, after he had lived there for several years in

meditation, a royal hunting party chased the hind into Giles' cave. One hunter shot an arrow into the thorn bush, hoping to hit the deer, but hit Giles in the leg instead, crippling him. The king sent doctors to care for his wound, and though Giles begged to be left alone, as Edinbuggers do, the king came often to see him.

Years after this, in their passage to Tyburn for execution, convicts were allowed to stop at Saint Giles' Hospital where they were presented with a bowl of ale called Saint Giles' Bowl: 'thereof to drink at their pleasure, as their last refreshing in this life,' and probably the only example in history of an Edinbugger giving away free drink. Once in Scotland during the seventeenth century his relics were stolen from a church and a huge rammy ensued. But they put them back anyway.

St Mungo, the other guy on the roof, and just a tad more choosy, is patron saint of Glasgow and salmon, giving him time to chill a bit and get on with Glasgow's coat of arms, which includes a bird, a fish, a bell and a tree, the symbols of Kentigern, one of his alternative monikers.

The bird commemorates the pet robin owned by Saint Serf, which was accidentally killed by monks who blamed it on Saint Kentigern. Saint Kentigern took the bird in his hands and prayed over it, restoring it to life.

The fish was one caught by Saint Kentigern in the Clyde. When it was slit open, a ring belonging to the Queen of Cadzow was miraculously found inside it. The Queen was suspected of intrigue by her husband, who also accused her of knocking off his ring. She had asked Saint Kentigern for help, and he found and restored the ring in this way to clear her name.

The bell may have been given to Saint Kentigern by the Pope. The original bell, which was tolled at funerals, no longer exists and was replaced by the magistrates of Glasgow in 1641. The bell of 1641 is preserved in the People's Palace.

The tree is symbol of an incident in Saint Kentigern's childhood. Left in charge of the holy fire in Saint Serf's monastery, he fell asleep and the fire went out. However he broke off some frozen branches from a hazel tree and miraculously re-kindled the fire.

Mungo, by the way, means *'darling'*. See friendly, see Weegies?

18
A MORAL

The Weegie teacher gave her class an exercise – get their parents to tell them a story with a moral.

The next day the kids came back and one by one began to tell their stories.

'Johnny, do you have a story to share?'

'Yes, miss, my daddy told me a story about my Auntie Mel. Auntie Mel was a pilot in Iraq and her plane was hit. She had to bail out over enemy territory and all she had was two bottles of Buckfast, a gun and a survival knife. She drank the Buckie on the way down so it would not break and then her parachute landed her right in the middle of twenty enemy troops. She shot fifteen of them with the gun until she ran out of bullets and killed four more with the knife till the blade broke and then she killed the last Iraqi with her bare hands and her teeth, biting his throat out.'

'Jesus!' said the horrified teacher. 'What kind of moral did your daddy tell you from that horrible story?'

Johnny replied, 'Stay well away from Auntie Mel when she's been drinking.'

20
ERUDITE INSULTS

If you live in Glasgow, then being awake is not necessarily a desirable state.

In Glasgow, you're considered posh if you have slates on your roof. Indeed, if you have a roof.

If you take a picture of a Weegie, he runs about claiming you've stolen his soul.

21
DRY HUMOUR

Two Weegies are walking down Leith Walk when they see a sign in a shop window. Suits £15.00, shirts £2.00, trousers £2.50. One said to the other one, 'Look at that – we could buy a lot of that gear and, when we get back to Glasgow we could make a fortune. When we go into the shop don't say anything, let me do all the talking, cause if they hear our right accent they might not serve us, so I'll speak in my best Edinburgh voice.'

They go in and he orders, in his best attempt at a Fettes voice, 50 suits at £15.00, 100 shirts at £2.00 and 50 trousers at £2.50. The owner of the shop says, 'You two are Weegies, aren't you?'

The Weegie replies, 'Aye, OK pal, how the hell did you know that?'

The owner says, 'This is a dry cleaners.'

22

SEX, BUT NOT WITH COAL IN

Two brothers, both Edinbuggers, Nimmo and Farquahar, go into business together. At the end of the first year they try to balance their account books, but were £100 short. They tried again and again, but no matter which way they tried to do it, they always came out £100 short.

'Tell me the truth, Nimmo,' asked his brother, 'are you keeping a fancy woman on the side?'

23
LITTLE DARLINGS

Little Weegie Sandy walked into the house shortly before noon.

'Sandy!' his mother cried. 'What are you doing home from school so early?'

'I got the right answer to the question.'

Beaming, his mother asked, 'Which question was that?'

'Who put the dog shite on the teacher's chair. It was me.'

24
SAY WHAT?

Edinburgh saying
In Glasgow, talk is cheap, because supply exceeds demand.

Edinburgh question
What do you call a Weegie woman with one leg? Eileen.

25
STILL GAME

The prosecution and defence had both presented their final arguments in a case involving a Weegie accused of operating an illegal still. The judge turned to the jury and asked, 'Before giving you your instructions, do any of you have any questions?'

'Yes, M'lud,' replied one of the jurors, a fellow schemie. 'Did the defendant boil the malt one or two hours, how does he cool it quickly, and at what point does he add the yeast?'

26
DUMB WEEGIES

Edinbugger: 'Did you ever hear that joke about the museum in Edinburgh that had a skull of Mary Queen of Scots when she was twelve in one room, and a skull when she was thirty in another?'

'Naw,' said the Weegie. 'What was it?'

Jimmy and Jock went into their pub in Possil in great good humour and ordered two large whiskies.

'Are you boays celebrating something?' asked the bartender.

'We ur,' said Jimmy. 'We've just finished a jigsaw puzzle in record time. A hundred pieces it hud, and it only took us six months.'

'Six months? But that's quite a long time,' said the bartender.

'I don't hink so,' said Donald. 'It said on the box, three to five years.'

27
GOLF

'Sandy, you promised to be home at two o'clock this afternoon and now it's after six.'

'Bonny wife, please. That Weegie I drew in the Medal is dead – dropped dead on the 4th green this morning at St. Andrews.'

'Oh, how terrible.'

'It certainly was. The whole day it's been, hit the ball . . . drag the Weegie . . . hit the ball . . . drag the Weegie.'

28
LOTHIAN'S FINEST

One of Lothians' finest pulls over a Weegie who's been weaving in and out of the lanes. He goes up to the man's window and says, 'Sir, I need you to blow into this breathalyzer tube.'

The man says, 'Sorry, orifice, I can't do that. I am an asthmatic. If I do that, I'll have a really bad asthma attack.'

'Okay, fine. I need you to come down to the station to give a blood sample.'

'I can't do that either. I am a haemophiliac. If I do that, I'll bleed to death.'

'Well, then, we need a urine sample.'

'I'm sorry, officer, I can't do that either. I am also a diabetic. If I do that, I'll get really low blood sugar.'

'All right, then I need you to come out here and walk this white line.'

'I can't do that either, orifice.'

'Why not?'

'Because I'm absolutely fuckin' steamin'.'

A Weegie lay sprawled across three entire seats in the Royal Lyceum Theatre.

When the usher came by and noticed this, he whispered to the man, 'Sorry, sir, but you're only allowed one seat.'

The man heard and looked up, but didn't budge.

The usher became impatient. 'Sir, if you don't get up from there I'm going to have to call the manager.'

This time the man made a gutteral sound, a very Weegie noise, which infuriated the usher, who turned and marched briskly back up the aisle in search of his manager. In a few moments, both the usher and the manager returned and stood over the man. Together the two of them tried repeatedly to move him, but with no success.

Finally, they summoned the police.

The large sub-unit of Lothian's finest surveyed the situation briefly then asked, 'All right, my friend, what's your name?'

'Jimmy,' the man muttered.

'Oho,' said the cop, having detected the Weegie accent. 'Where are you from, Jimmy?'

With pain in his voice Jimmy replied, 'The balcony.'

Late one Friday night the policeman spotted a Glasgow man driving very erratically through the streets of Edinburgh. They pulled the man over and asked him if he had been drinking that evening.

'Aye, I have. It's Friday, you know, and I'm in a foreign city, so I stopped by a pub where I had six or seven pints. And then there was something called 'Happy Hour' and they served these huge voddies for buttons. I had four or five ae them. Then I stopped on the way home to get another bottle for later. I've drunk some already.' And the man fumbled around in his jacket until he located his bottle of vodka, which he held up for inspection.

The officer sighed, and said, 'Sir, I'm afraid I'll need you to step out of the car and take a breathalyser test.'

The Weegie said indignantly, 'How? Dae ye no believe me?'

29
A WEE BIT OF HISTORY

In olden times it was customary for couples contemplating marriage to pay a visit to Parliament Close in Edinburgh. This was the home of the capital city's silversmiths, where the bride and groom would select their silver spoons, then just as important as a part of any marriage as the ring, cake and bridesmaids. Usually two journeys were made involving the silver spoons. The first, a few weeks before the ceremony, to select the spoons and give details of the initials to be marked on them, the other to receive and pay for the spoons.

Then the Weegies stole them.

30
WEEGIE EDUCATION

DRAFT HIGHER GRADE
MODERN MATHEMATICS PAPER 2006

HIGHLY CONFIDENTIAL

GLASGOW REGION

Name ....

Nickname ....

Gangname ....

Question 1

Shuggie the Stakey has bought half a kilo of cocaine for large. He wants to make 300% on the deal and still pay Mad Malky his 10% protection money. How much must he charge for a gram?

Question 2

Wee Davie reckons he'll get £42.50 extra Marriage Allowance a week if he ties the knot with Fat Alice. Even if he steals the ring, the wedding will cost him

£587. And he'll have to start buying two fish suppers every night instead of one. How long will it be before Davie wishes he'd stayed single?

Question 3

When Rangers play Celtic, their fans sing 'The Sash' every 10 minutes when they're winning and every 15 minutes when they're losing. How many times did they sing it last season?

Question 4

Joey and Davie stole a 1999 green Toyota 1600GL with 35,000 miles on the clock – and got a grand for it. How much more would they have got if it had been metallic silver, done 29,000 miles and had low profile tyres?

Question 5

Jake the Flake and Fingers got grassed up for dealing speed. The Flake got 18 months but Fingers got 3 years. How many more previous convictions did Fingers have?

EXTRA CREDIT: Who was Fingers' brief?

31
TO BE SURE, TO BE SURE

Three men are sitting in the maternity ward of a hospital waiting for the imminent birth of their respective children. One is an Edinbugger, one a Weegie and the other a West Indian. They are all very nervous and pacing the floor – as you do in these situations.

Suddenly the doctor bursts through the double doors saying, 'Gentlemen you won't believe this but your wives have all had their babies within five minutes of each other.'

The men are beside themselves with happiness and joy. 'And,' said the doctor, 'they have all had little boys.' The fathers are ecstatic and congratulate each other over and over. 'However, we do have one slight problem,' the doctor said. 'In all the confusion we may have mixed the babies up getting them to the nursery and would be grateful if you could join us there to try and help identify them.'

With that the Edinbugger raced past the doctor and bolted to the nursery. Once inside he picked up a dark skinned infant with dreadlocks saying: 'There's no doubt about it, this boy is mine!'

The doctor looked bewildered and said: 'Well sir, of all the babies, I would have thought that maybe this child could be of West Indian descent.'

'That's a maybe,' said the Edinbugger, 'but one of the other two is a Weegie and I'm not taking the risk!'

32
FOOTBALL

The Post Office has just recalled their latest stamps. They had pictures of Old Firm players on them and people couldn't work out which side to spit on.

What's the difference between Barry Ferguson and God?

God doesn't think he's Barry Ferguson.

Barry Ferguson walks into a pub with a pile of dog shite in his hand and says, 'Look what I nearly stood in!'

Everybody in Scottish football hates the Old Firm, as Celtic and Rangers have been called since clichés were invented. Here is an Edinburgh song about one of them. At the time of writing Celtic were 5-0 down in the first leg against that giant of European football, Artmedia Bratislava.

Where Everybody Knows Your Game

Tune: Where Everybody Knows Your Name

Making your way in Europe today
  takes everything you've got.
Sixty thousand diddies wi' season tickets bought,
But mebbe ye huv tae win a game,
In order to progress,
A bit beyond the second round,
Where bams like you are never found.
It's just another fact of life.
It's never gonny go away.
There's nae Tims left in Europe on Christmas Day.

It's a grand old team to play for,
  or so we're fucking told.
Yet every year in Europe there's eleven jerseys sold.
Tae hasbeen shites fae France or Spain,
Who just can't believe their luck,
When yer name comes oot the hat,
Tae cries of, 'Who the fuck is that?'
You're just a pishy Glasgow team.
You gie us a' the boke.
Yer European campaign's a fucking joke.

33
YOU KNOW THAT YOU ARE LIVING IN A GLASGOW SCHEME WHEN

Your standard of living improves when you go camping.

Your neighbour has asked to borrow half a can of beer.

None of the tyres on your van are the same size.

You can get heroin delivered.

Your binman is confused about what goes and what stays.

You actually wear shoes your dog brought home.

You've been in a punch-up at a jumble sale.

You carry a baseball bat in the front seat of your van so you can pacify the weans in the back.

You make a phone call and the answering machine message in Possil says: 'If you don't need to buy smack and it is just dope you want, press the hash key.'

34

THE NED CAPITAL OF THE WORLD:

GLASGOW NEDOPOLIS – A NEDUCATION

Glasgow invented the ned, though they are not expecting a Queen's Award. Edinburgh always gets the queens' award. Along with McEwans, neddism is one of Glasgow's more famous exports. Here are a few facts and fictions to enable you to survive the cradle of neddery.

The first thing you must know about is Ned Viagra. You just think you're hard. No, just joking. They use Buckfast.

I am indebted to a website www.glasgowsurvival.co.uk for a great deal of this information. Its operator prefers, understandably if you have seen it, to remain anonymous.

Lifestyle Etiquette for Neds
Neds and Nedettes. On public transport always remember – SHOUT, don't talk.

And don't forget the 1-fuck-to-3 rule. For every

three words SHOUTED, one of them must be 'fuck' or one of its grammatical derivatives – fucked, fucking, fucker, any of these will do fine. If you follow these two simple rules your friends will think you are just 'awesome'. Passengers outside your extremely narrow age group, however, will simply think you're a bunch of loud-mouthed fannies and will want to take a chainsaw to your extremities.

Diddies Dress Code, Dictionary, and Rules

The tribe of neds, aka the Burberry apes, can be divided into a number of different types, most of which are described below.

The Common Ned

The common ned, as the name suggests, is the most common type you will come across in Glasgow. This widespread ned will invariably be kitted out in a brightly coloured track suit, which serves as a warning to decent folk to stay away, much like the stripes of a wasp. Another trait borrowed from the animal kingdom is the almost perpendicular cap angle, which can be equated to an animal's instinctual response to a threat which may include ears pointing upwards, tail erect, or feathers cocked.

To continue the animal analogy, these neds will travel in packs, and feel uncomfortable not doing so, though you will see many scattered all over the place, not unlike a plague of rats.

The trackies will be tucked into bright white socks stuffed into dazzlingly colourful trainers. Their pack culture gives them more confidence to harass members of the general public and if you see a troop of neds in the street or in a bus shelter or in a local park you may well become a target for their abuse and you may well hear such phrases as, 'You're a pure poofy wee prick,' or 'Look at the state ay you ya dobber,' (a particularly ironic one). These phrases vary greatly and it is rare to hear the same line more than once from the same ned.

The Dressed Ned

It should be mentioned that it is rare to find a common ned over the age of 18. When a common ned gets old enough they will no longer wish to hang about in a bus shelter and they will usually graduate to become a 'Dressed Ned'. These neds can be seen in abundance on a Friday or Saturday night in Glasgow city centre. They will usually be wearing clothes which on average would have come to over £300, not including the tanning parlour fee. They will go to places like The Moon, Archaos, Destiny, the Savoy, Victoria's or Walkabout, among others, which is not to say that any of these estimable establishments encourage ned behaviour. Far from it. If you wish to see some of these neds but don't wish to go to any of their places you may find it fruitful to hang around the streets at 3am on a weekend night and watch them fight and bottle each other until the sun comes up. The area at the intersection between Sauchiehall Street and Renfield Street is truly scumbag central between 2am and 4am every Friday and Saturday night. It is like a little Bermuda Triangle of clubs and it's a haven for the dressed ned.

The Beggar Ned

Glasgow just wouldn't be Glasgow without the good old beggar ned. These neds make a (fairly healthy) living out of simply asking people for money in the street. If you give them the money they ask for they won't sing you a song, they won't do you a dance and they probably won't even thank you. Their request for 20p will usually be accompanied by a heart-breaking story, but don't worry because the story isn't actually true. Perhaps if they toned it down a bit and made it more believable people would be fooled more often but then intelligence is not an attribute of the beggar ned. These neds will generally look and smell similar to a common ned, but only if you took the common ned and rolled him in muck for a day or two then urinated on him.

The Wee Cheeky Ned

All neds have big mouths, and many are cheeky, but the Cheeky Ned is an astonishingly impudent breed of ned, easily differentiated from the more common varieties. The purveyor of many a mischievous comment, this ned is full of disrespect for and defiance towards everyone and everything. Below average height, with a face permanently bearing an unsettlingly impish grin, and a voice as yet unbroken, these tykes can be extremely irritating. And this irritation is amplified by the fact you can do absolutely nothing about it. Whenever you spot one, the chances are they will be surrounded by a scattering of Common Neds and a 'Goon Ned'. It is this ned-curtain that gives them the courage to speak out at anything, and instils in them their legendary defiance. When surrounded by their own kind, these neds fear nothing. They will mock any authority, whether it is a security guard or a train-driver, and square up to people twice their size, separating them from their more common cousins whose cheekiness is largely incidental. So, if you ever trip up in the street in front of a squad of neds and a mocking, shrill scream followed by elaborate impressions of you replaces the more common, 'Ha ha, look at you, ya nugget,' you'll know that the troop was blessed with a cheeky ned.

The Mad Ned

This ned is quite rare, and will, more often than not, travel alone. The Mad Ned is very dangerous, and if spotted, must be avoided. Do not confuse this type of ned with the typical hard man of a ned troop. The garden variety hard-man's tough guy image is merely an act of machismo, and will in most cases disappear along with his squad. The Mad Ned is a highly anti-social individual without a twinge of humanity who, when travelling with a squad, is the one described by his pals as having 'taken it too far', whether that be kicking a man to death, or introducing a cat to a firework. So, wherever a ned squad goes too far, a Mad Ned was travelling with them. Ordinary neds themselves fear them, and behave like sycophants around them.

More commonly, however, perhaps resulting from a slightly psychotic nature, they travel alone, with the aim of destroying people and property. Many have graced our televisions in programmes showing CCTV footage – the man, seemingly without purpose, walking down the street at 2am damaging car after car; the unprovoked attack on a passer-by culminating in several stamps to the head; those curious individuals who push a blade into an innocent bystander for no other reason than they were there at the time. He is unable to inhibit impulses in the brain like the rest of us can. If this ned has a golf club, he will swing it whether he is playing golf or not.

The Goon Ned

Any ned squad worth their kappas has a resident Goon Ned, an oversized, vacant eyed galoot of sub-normal intelligence. Their purpose is appealingly simple – the physical protection of the squad. Where there are power vacancies within a squad, this ned will often take charge, a result of his physical prowess rather than his intellectual shrewdness. On the whole, however, the slightly smaller in stature hard man will take charge, and the Goon Ned will usually stick to what he's good at. Though these neds are easy to outwit, and it may be tempting to when face-to-chest with one, it isn't really worth a black eye, which is what you'll get, as physical aggression is the Goon Ned's answer to everything.

The Senga Ned

Like primitive tribes from Stone Age times, each squad of neds will have their resident 'senga neds'. These female neds are quite distinctive in appearance. Senga neds wear pretty much the same clothes as the male neds when they are hanging around the streets or in bus stops, although this can dramatically change to pretty much no clothes if they are planning a trip to a club. They are usually covered in bright gold jewellery and sporting gold name tags around their necks. People have been debating for years whether these name tags are to remind the senga of their name or to remind the male neds of the group what one he's 'doin'' that night. Senga neds will also sport an abnormal number of gold chains round their necks along with a huge collection of variously aged and hued love bites. About half of all senga neds can be seen in the street usually pushing a pram with a number of children in it. There will be a jacket hanging on one handle of the pram and a Farmfoods bag underneath it. No one knows what's in the Farmfoods bag. Spotting a senga ned in the street isn't very hard as they are usually heard before they are seen. It is common to hear a piercing shrill a couple of streets away indicating that a senga ned is mad at one of her males or an innocent girl who was passing by. Examples of the cries you may hear are – 'Av goat tae bring up four weans oan ma ain while yoor oot shaggin,' or 'Whit the fuck were ye lookin at ma man fur ya nugly cow.' An aggressive senga is not a pretty sight so it's not advisable to approach one in the street at any time.

The Friendly Ned

This is a highly controversial ned to include but it has been spotted enough times to warrant an inclusion in this list. The Friendly Ned is a rare creature. It is unlikely that the Friendly Ned will exist in its own right. It is more likely that a friendly ned is simply a common ned when he is in a squad of neds but transforms into a friendly ned when he is on his own. The Friendly Ned will usually be found on public transport and although it can seem slightly intimidating when they initially approach you, it soon becomes obvious that this ned doesn't actually want to take your money or call you a dafty. He simply wants to participate in an irreverent conversation about football, drinking or fighting. These neds are not very dangerous but it may happen that occasionally when you have been engaged in a conversation with one of them that another common ned may approach causing a change in the friendly back to a common ned, so they should be treated with caution. Friendly Neds will usually always be male neds. It is extremely rare to find a friendly senga ned.

The Family Man Ned

This ned is predominantly found outside of the city centre. He will usually be seen making his way down the road pushing a pram, with at least two other small children trailing behind, on his way to the DSS. These children will almost certainly be fighting with each other or throwing stones at buses and so the Family Man Ned will usually be shouting at them – 'Michela, stoap flingin stanes at Charlene.' This ned is slightly older than the other neds as he will have at least three children and can be considered as a good example of what happens to a young common ned who does not grow out of neddism. A ned can become trapped inside ned circles if he gets lumbered with a wean, turning into a family man ned, usually at the ages of 13 to 15.

The Cruiser Ned

It is unusual to find this ned outside a car unless he is being questioned by the police and they are usually only seen from chest level up wearing a Burberry baseball cap. These cruiser neds are dedicated to making their cars look as stupid as possible and they regularly congregate in public parks and on waste ground to show off how stupid the cars look and how many unnecessary things they have added to their 'motors' that week. These neds spend a lot of money to pursue their hobby and so will protect their cars with their life so it is not advisable to do anything to their cars other than point and laugh.

Some people may get mixed up between a Cruiser Ned and a Common Ned in a clapped out Nova. The main difference between the two is that a Cruiser Ned will travel in circles for a whole night pumping crap music out of the window, whereas a Common Ned in a Nova will drive fast for a night then set fire to the car.

The Working Ned

This is quite an unusual ned as they are not work shy in the slightest and will work full time hours like the rest of us. They do though, as you would imagine, bring their own touch of nedness to the working environment. The most common type of Working Ned is the one who gets on a bus in the morning – always the bus, even if a better transport option is available they will get on the bus – and head straight to the back to smoke a fag and discuss the weekend's football/fighting/drinking with his Working Ned friends. As this ned passes on the bus you will observe a glass bottle of Irn Bru and a *Sun/Daily Record* rolled up and in his back pocket and those big dirty brown boots with the woollen top on them that they all wear but aren't sold anywhere. Another type of Working Ned is the Office Ned. These Working Neds are not as obvious as the other kind as they are usually required to conform to the shirt and tie dress codes but you can spot one of these Working Neds by a sly pair of Burberry socks or a cap that comes off before the office is entered. These neds will also usually drive a car with unnecessary things attached to it and will bomb it into and out of the office car park in a show of neddism.

For many years Glaswegians have been wielding weapons, and it really is surprising how big a variety of weapons there are. Weegies are true geniuses at inventing things which they will use to hit or generally damage other people.

Since there are so many different types of object used to hit people, various words have emerged to describe each sub-division of weapon. The word 'chib' is used to describe cutting and slicing weapons, generally used on the face and head. The word 'cosh' or 'tool' is used to describe blunt objects such as a plank or a hammer. Long stabbing blades are referred to as 'stakeys' and screwdrivers and other thin stabbing implements are called 'spikes'. Weapons which encompass more than one category, such as small hatchets, are usually referred to as 'choppers'. Although each team will have their own nomenclature to describe each weapon, the terms described above are general for just about all teams throughout Glasgow. It is essential to get the nomenclature correct as a mugger with a stakey may well be offended if he was accused of chibbing you. And you don't want a ned with a stakey to be angry with you.

Of course there are hybrid weapons which encompass the hitting power of a cosh and the stabbing action of a stakey. Only a Weegie could come up with the hammer with a Stanley knife taped to the top. Genius!

The common ned in the street will generally be carrying only a common everyday knife. These are sometimes used for stabbing but they are mostly used to scare the people they are mugging, though it must be said that a ned will always be carrying a Buckfast bottle and this can become a default tool if one is needed.

If you come across a pack of rioting neds they will usually be carrying chibs, tools and probably even some spikes. Anything can become a weapon in this situation. Tables and chairs can and will be used as tools.

If you are out late at night in Glasgow, just in time for the clubs to empty, you may come across some dressed neds wielding glass bottles. These are initially used as tools but as soon as they break they become stakeys.

If you listen carefully you can often hear neds bragging that they have a machete or a sword in the 'hoose'. One ned who was assaulted with a sword was asked by the police to describe the weapon. He looked puzzled and said (through his nose), 'It wis jist an ordinary sword.' He lives in a society where swords are ordinary.

Dealing with Neds

If one says, 'Yer maw,' then reply, 'She died in a car crash last week.' It might shut him up, but don't expect shame or an apology.

Here is some advice and some words of wisdom from a serving beat polis, who also wishes to remain anonymous. I've tidied up his spelling and grammar. Tut, tut Officer.

Glasgow and Edinburgh neds are distinguishable in a couple of ways. Glasgow neds (e.g. Posso Yung Teem) for some reason tuck their trackies into their socks. Edinburgh neds (Niddrons from Niddry) wear no gold as they've pawned it for heroin. While the Weegie ned usually drinks Lanarkshire's favourite monks' brew, Buckfast, the Edinbugger ned has a choice and plumps for a mix of White Lightning and Mad Dog. This moves towards WKD or Smirnoff Ice as a leg opener on a Friday in downtown Leith.

However, we must understand a bit of the ned. They have nothing to lose and this is why they will often 'have a go' with anyone, including 6'2" Moshers*. Despite the balanced and nutritious mix of alcohol and prescribed and non-prescribed medication, the ned always manages to defend his honour. But if you 'have a go' the ned usually runs off or throws bricks (half-Niddrys in Embra) from a distance. Having a go is only advisable if you do have a much bigger knife than the ned, which is not always the case. One of the favourite parts of street policing is crossing swords (*Editor: not yet, not yet, dear God*) with neds, as it is too easy. Old-style beat officers would often carry ten large ball-bearings in police issue gloves with one ball in each finger. On approaching neds they'd gently swipe the glove towards them glancing the head/temple. This to their mates looks like nothing, but the poor ned has just been scudded in the heid with a bag of steel marbles. This doesn't half make the ned look stupid squealing in pain as the happy beat officer heads off whistling, PC Murdoch style.

*Mosher is a term used to describe a person who participates in the Mosh Pit at a rock concert, i.e., jumping and/or bumping into other members of the audience.

And a quote from a chap with a solution, possibly a bit of a harsh one.

Why is the stock response from these shitbags, when you square up to them, "When my uncle gets out the jail, you're getting yer jaw rattled," or "Do you know who my da is?" always shouted at you as they beat an undignified retreat. A reply of, "Yes, Julian Clary," is advisable here. I still see red whenever I see shell suits, skip caps and swaggers. We really should just take matters into our own hands, as no-one else will, and start stringing them up from lamposts. It's the only solution.

On a different note, I was walking past Borders Bookstore in Buchanan St, that well known skag-dealing and magazine-selling area. One of the living-dead harpies was talking to some raggedy-arsed male wreckage, moaning about the police, etc. On bidding them farewell, she told them to, "Be lucky." I still laugh about it, albeit in a callous, heartless, spiteful way.

And an anecdote from another encounter.

For a few years I was a security officer in a large retail store, which must remain nameless (and is directly opposite Buchanan Bus Station).

Due to the neds mistaking the store for a re-fuelling station on their way from their high flat nests in Toonheed down to Virgin and HMV, security had to man the doors at all times.

One day a perfect specimen of a 'sparkle heid'* came into the store, looking around in that unmistakeable furtive manner. On eventually spotting me in my bright green security uniform, standing ten yards in front of him, he jumped like a scalded cat, as if seeing a security guy in the store was the very last thing he expected. Having regained his composure (as much com-posure as you can regain dressed in a Kappa suit) he approached and the talking bit started.

'Oi mate. Says yuv goat a shirt anat oot ra store but yuv no goat a receipt right? Any hashle getting yur money fur it, anat, ye no?'

I was about to say no problem, sir, as long as the shirt is in the same condition blah, blah. But thought better of it.

'Are you telling me that you have a shirt out of our store, and you want to return it for a refund, and you don't have a receipt?'

'Eeeehhh! No yet.'

'Right! Out! And don't come back, bird brain.' And as I 'escort' him through the revolving doors, the inevitable parting shot:

'Aw right wee man. Shtay cool. Nae hashle man. For fuck sake ya dobber. Ahm reporting you ya cunt, an ahm no comin back here ahl tell yae. Away an fuck the lot of yez.'

*sparkle heid : A distinctive type of ned, so called because of a particularly bright 'sparkly' look about the eyes. This is caused by a regular concoction of seriously illegal drugs washed down with Buckie. After a few weeks of continued abuse the ned works out the combination that keeps him awake and 'no pukin'.

And another solution.

Legalised Ned Hunting

We can advertise and promote to all would-be big game hunters. At £10,000 a bullet the Scottish Parliament could use the cash to subsidise the cost of the average ned/senga seven child family, until through natural selection they themselves become the endangered species. Survival of the fittest would never become more relevant. How many Buckie drinkers can outrun an open top Jeep with four overweight Americans equipped with sniper rifles and a highly paid local guide?

Rules
1. Anything in Kappa, Burberry etc is fair game.
2. See Rule 1

Benefits
Within two to four years large sections of Scotland would be open to all once more. JJB Sports, Sports Division etc, would all close and Income and Council Tax will reduce.

Or possibly
Far from being a blight on our communities a ned can both brighten our cities and educate our children, provided of course we have suitable containment. We would be able to surround them with high voltage enclosures such as those being used at Barlinnie. Visitors to the attraction would be able to see wild herds of the Common Ned hanging around at the base of authentically re-built housing blocks or trying to make wee rollies whilst swigging MD 20 20 at bus stops. Tours would be conducted in the shells of burnt-out police cars so as not to attract the attentions of the neds. If, however, a tourist were approached by any of the neds, the burnt-out police cars would be equipped with sound recordings of a school. This being the most alien of all sounds to a ned, he would be temporally confused and need a fix

of spray solvent to help clear his mind.

There would be gift shops with shuttered windows and screens in-front of the counters to enable young Cheeky Neds to mingle with tourists and staff, staff would be Working Neds and heavily pregnant Nedettes, all trained to serve with an air of contempt for being made to do anything. Tourists and staff would have toilet facilities provided on every vertical concrete surface and any secluded passageways between shops or buildings. Attached to the safari part of the attraction would be a fun park offering a full range of Ned pastimes. The choices of activities would include – driving around slowly listening to anything sub 20 hertz, allowing the squeaky whine of your Cruiser Ned guide to be heard above the pounding bass, and driving around quickly as above, but trying to throw all contraband 'oot yer windae' before the police catch up with you. If you were to favour more intellectual pursuits there would be daily games of *Who Wants To Be a Millionaire: The Benefits Edition* and *The Weakest Genetic Link*.

All patrons would receive lasting memories of their trip in the form of either a facial stab wound, severe tooth and gum disease, acute cholesterol problems and a photograph taken at the moment their first hit off the crack-pipe took effect.

And some news nedlines

Q. What is the difference between a dying ned and an onion?
A. Onions make you cry.

Q. Why are neds like slinkies?
A. They have no real use but it's great to watch one fall down a flight of stairs.

Q. What do you call a Nedette in a white tracksuit?
A. The bride.

Q. What's the difference between a ned and a coconut?
A. One's thick and hairy, the other's a coconut.

Q. How do you get 100 neds into a phone box?
A. Paint three stripes on it.

Q. Two neds in a car without any music. Who's driving?
A. The police.

35
IF STAR WARS WAS SET IN GLASGOW

Darth Vader would referred to as, 'Auld Helmet Heid' or in moments of stress, 'That Dome-Heided Basturd.'

Chewbacca would look roughly the same except he'd only be about 5ft tall, from Blackhill and called Shug. He'd have the same amount of body hair but would also have tattoos, would permanently smell of drink and sport a Rangers top.

Obi-Wan Kenobi would invariably be referred to as Chief or Big Yin by his cohorts. People trying to start a fight with him would address him as Jobby Wanky-Nobby.

R2D2 would refuse to go out on the streets after 10pm because of the number of drunks who would try to stuff chip papers in his head casing or piss on him. He would also refuse to go near groups of wee boys at any time because of the high risk of being spray painted or dumped in front of a speeding train or set on fire.

Although proficient in over 3500 languages C3Po would still be unable to understand anything anyone from the East End of Glasgow said. He would regularly get beaten up for being a 'greetin-faced poof fae Milngavie.'

The Millenium Falcon would have static strips, tinted windscreens and extra-flared exhaust ports. It would have a *Daily Record* 'I Love Scotland' sticker in the back window and a Saltire bumper sticker.

Princess Leia would get captured by Darth Vader because it's hard to run very fast when you're wearing 5 inch platform heels and a tiny silver mini-skirt which keeps hiking up over your arse every two steps. And you've been a heavy smoker since you were six.

The best way to destroy the Death Star would not turn out to be a desperate all-out attack. Two easy ways would be – alter its orbit so it passed through Bridgeton and tell the locals it was full of kafflicks, or leave it unattended in Easterhouse.

Lines from the film as they would be uttered in the vernacular
Han Solo
'I've got a real bad feeling about this.'
'Ah'm shitin' masel' here, boy.'

'Bring 'em on! I prefer a straight fight to all this sneaking around.'
'Come right ahead then, cunts! Fight the fucking lot o' ye!'

'There's no mystical energy field controls my destiny.'
'The Force? Dae youse think ah came doon wi the rain?'

'Hokey religions and ancient weapons are no match for a good blaster at your side, kid.'
'Nae messin aboot wi the god squad and auld rubbish, wee man. Get yersel' a decent shooter.'

Darth Vader (trying to shoot down Luke Skywalker)
'The Force is strong in this one.'
'Stop shooglin', ya wee bastard.'

Princess Leia
'You're a little short for a Stormtrooper aren't you?'
'Ah didny think they took shoart-erses in the polis.'

'This bucket of bolts is never going to get us past that blockade.'
'Wuv goat NAE chance in this pile o' shite.'

Admiral Motti
'Don't try to frighten us with your sorcerer's ways, Lord Vader.'

'*You think you're that hard Vader, so ye dae. Well, we're no feart ae you!*'

Obi Wan

'I felt a great disturbance in the Force.'
'*Fuck me! Whit wiz aw that?*'

Luke to the Emperor

'Your overconfidence is your weakness.'
'*Oh ye bloody think so. I'll make you feel the fucking Force pal!*'

36
GLASGOW BANTER

Q. What's the first question at a Glasgow pub quiz?
A. What are you looking at?

Q. Why does the River Clyde run through Glasgow?
A. Because if it walked it would be mugged.

Q. What do you call a Weegie in a three-bedroom semi?
A. A burglar.

Q. What do you say to a Weegie in a uniform?
A. Big Mac & Fries, please.

To a Fringe audience
'Have you all switched off your mobile phones? And have the people from Glasgow turned off their electronic tags?'

Weegies consider themselves well dressed if their socks match.

37
WARNING

'He needed killin',' is a valid defence in Glasgow courts.

A few things Edinbuggers shouldn't to say to a Weegie cop when stopped for speeding

I can't reach my licence unless you hold my Bolly.

Sorry officer, I didn't realize my radar detector wasn't plugged in.

You must have been doing 125 to keep up with me, excellent driving.

I thought you had to be in relatively good physical shape to be a police officer.

I pay your wages, old boy.

Great officer, that's terrific. The last monkey only gave me a warning as well.

I was trying to keep up with traffic. Yes, I know there are no other cars about, that's how far they are ahead of me.

What do you mean, 'Have I been drinking?' You're the trained specialist.

38
STRATHCLYDE'S FINEST

On Christmas morning a polis on horseback in Maryhill, heading for the major Christmas present resettlement area that is Possil, is sitting at a traffic light and next to him is a wee boy on a shiny new bike. The cop says to the kid, 'Nice bike you've got there. Did Santa steal that for you?' The boy says, 'Aye.' The cop says, 'Well, next year tell Santa to put a light on that bike.' The cop then proceeds to issue the kid a bicycle safety order, meaning that he has to turn up at the police station. The boy takes the chit and before he rides off says, 'By the way, that's a nice horse you've got there. Did Santa bring that to you?' Humouring the kid, the polis says, 'Aye, that he did.' The boy says, 'Well, next year tell Santa to put the prick underneath the horse.'

Strathclyde Police, MI5, and a secret Government department are all trying to prove that they are the best at apprehending criminals. Tony Blair decides to give them a test. He releases a rabbit into a forest and each of them has to catch it.

MI5 goes in. They place animal informants throughout the forest. They question all plant and mineral witnesses. After three months of extensive investigations they conclude that rabbits do not exist.

The ultra-secret Government department goes in. After two weeks with no success they poison the forest with some mysterious substance, killing nearly everything in it, and they make no apologies. Nobody ever mentions their failure. Or their existence. A bit like Masons in the police force.

Strathclyde's finest go in. They come out two hours later with a Rottweiller that is showing a bit of wear and tear. It is limping on all four legs and pissing blood, but there are of course no visible injuries.

The dog is yelling, 'Okay! Okay! I'm a rabbit! I'm a rabbit!'

39
SCHOOL TALES, TALL AND TRUE

Somewhere in darkest Glasgow, an Attendance Officer accompanied by a Depute Head (safety in numbers) went into a block of flats to speak to a family about the daughter's poor attendance.

As they climbed the stairs they spotted a large Rottweiler patrolling the landing outside the flat they were going to visit. Undaunted by this slavering beast, they rang the bell. The door was opened and in rushed the dog. They were greeted by the mother and taken into the barely furnished living room.

The conversation wasn't going too well and to make matters worse, the DHT saw the dog cock its leg and pee up against a wall in the room. Nobody said anything and he decided to keep quiet.

The conversation became more heated and then he saw the dog do a shit in the corner. Again nobody mentioned it.

Eventually the Attendance Officer decided to call a halt to the meeting as the family were becomingly increasingly hostile towards their callers.

They were shown out somewhat abruptly and

started to walk downstairs, both glad to have escaped, when the flat door was thrown open and the father shouted after them:

'An' youse can take yer fucking dog wae ye!'

A school outing to the east coast was the first time for many out of Glasgow. 'What's that big puddle over there, sur?'

'The North Sea, James.'

One day a Weegie boy went into his Classics class and placed a lump of rock on his teacher's desk. When the teacher asked where this rock had come from, the pupil replied, 'It's a present frae my big brother (a former pupil). He was in Greece wae the army and he chipped a bit aff the Parthenon fur ye!'

In a recent written Home Economics test in Glasgow on cookery, the pupils were asked to write down the names of three typical Scottish dishes.

One pupil carefully wrote, 'A plate, a cup and a saucer.'

40
DOGGED SUPER SALESMAN

When the shop manager of a large Edinburgh tailor's returned from lunch, he noticed that the Weegie sales assistant's hand was bandaged, but before he could ask about the bandage the guy said he had some very good news for him.

'Guess what?' he said. 'I finally sold that terrible suit we've had on the rack for so long.'

'Do you mean that repulsive pink-and-orange double-breasted monstrosity?' the manager asked.

'The very one.'

'That's brilliant,' the manager cried. 'I thought we'd never get rid of that horrible thing. That had to be the ugliest suit we've ever had. But why is your hand bandaged?'

The salesman replied, 'It was David Blunkett that bought it, and his guide dog bit me.'

41
ANOTHER GOOD DOG

Four men were bumming about how clever their dogs were. The first man was an Edinbugger engineer, the second man was an Edinbugger accountant, the third man was an Edinbugger chemist and the fourth was a Weegie schemie.

To show off, the engineer said to his dog, 'Protractor, do your trick.' Protractor trotted over to a desk, took out some paper and a pen, and promptly drew a circle, a square, and a triangle.

Everyone agreed that was pretty clever. However, the accountant said his dog could do better. He called his dog and said, 'Slide Rule, do your trick.' Slide Rule went into the kitchen, returned with a dozen biscuits and divided them into four equal piles of three each.

Everyone agreed that was pretty good, but the chemist said his dog could do better. He called his dog and said, 'Measure, do your trick.' Measure got up, walked to the fridge in the kitchen, took out a pint of milk, got a glass from the cupboard and poured exactly a half pint without spilling a drop.

Everyone agreed that was good. The three men turned to the Possil gadgie and said, 'What can your dog do?' He called to his dog and said, 'Catkiller, do your trick.' Catkiller jumped to his feet, ate the biscuits, drank the milk, peed on the paper, sexually assaulted the other three dogs, claimed he injured his back while doing so, filed a complaint about unsafe working conditions, put in for compen and went home on the Pat and Mick.

42
AND FINALLY, A LAST CALL

It was Weegie Pat's last day on the job after 35 years of carrying the post through all kinds of weather to the same neighbourhoods of Edinburgh. Everybody knew Weegie Pat, though they didn't of course speak to him much.

But surprise! When he arrived at the first house, he was greeted by the whole family there, who all hugged and congratulated him and sent him on his way with a cheque for £50.

At the second house they presented him with superb Cuban cigars in an 18-carat gold box, while the folk at the third house gave him a case of 30-year-old Dalmore.

At the fourth house he was met at the door by a stunning blonde in her lingerie. She took him by the arm and led him up the stairs to the bedroom where she blew his mind with the most passionate love he had ever experienced.

When he had had enough they went downstairs, where the woman made him a giant breakfast – eggs, tomatoes, bacon, sausage, beans, black pudding, the complete heart-stopper, and freshly-squeezed orange juice. When he was truly satisfied she poured him a cup of steaming coffee.

As she was pouring, he noticed a five pound note sticking out from under the cup's bottom edge. 'All this was just too wonderful for words,' he said, 'but what's the fiver for?'

'Well,' said the blonde, 'last night, I told my husband that today would be your last day, and that we should do something special for you. I asked him what to give you.

'He said, "Fuck him. Give him a fiver." The breakfast was my idea.'

Merr WEEGIES

vs.

Mair EDINBUGGERS

Merr 'friendly' rivalry
and getting into the Edinbuggers' mince

WEEGIES START HERE

25
PHILOSOPHY

An Edinbugger is a man who feels badly when he feels good for fear he'll feel worse when he feels better.

Showing-off is a hanging offence in Edinburgh.

How many Edinbuggers does it take to change a lightbulb?
  None, they form a self-help group called, 'How to cope with life in the dark.'

Glasgow saying: Life is shite. Get a fucking helmet, okay?

To the Glaswegian, the glass is half full.
To the Aberdonian, the glass is half empty.
To the Edinbugger, the glass is twice as big as it needs to be.

26
CANNIBALLOCKS

A Weegie, an Edinbugger and a Aberdonian were captured by cannibals. The chief comes to them and says, 'The bad news is that now we've caught you and we're going to kill you. We will put you in a pot, cook you, eat you and then we're going to use your skins to build a canoe. The good news is that you can choose how to die.'

The Edinbugger says, 'Give me a case of gin and a few bottles of tonic.' He then retires to his hut and after a few choruses of, 'Hibees till I die!' drinks himself to death and is duly skinned, cooked, eaten, and turned into a canoe.

The Aberdonian says, 'Brandy for me please, might as well go the expensive way. And a little ginger ale.' The chief gives him the brandy and the mixer, and after a few renditions of, 'The Dons for ever!' he duly expires and is skinned, cooked etc.

The Weegie says, 'Gies a crate of whisky and a fork. Nae watter necessary.' The chief is puzzled, but he shrugs and gives him the whisky and the fork. The Weegie takes them and goes to his hut. Later

the chief goes to see him and there he is, half of the whisky gone, broken bottle in one hand, fork in the other, jabbing himself all over . . . the stomach, the sides, the chest, everywhere. There is blood gushing out, it's horrible. The chief is appalled and asks, 'My God, what are you doing?'

And the Weegie responds, as he sticks the broken bottle in the chief's face, 'Fuck you AND your canoe!'

27
THE LORD GOD AND EDINBUGGERS

Eric the Edinbugger finds himself in dire trouble. His business has gone bust and he's got serious financial problems. He's so desperate that he decides to ask God for help. 'God, please help me. Ah've lost ma wee store and if ah dinnae get some money, ah'm going to lose my hoose too. Please let me win the lottery.'

Lottery night. Someone else wins.

Eric prays again. 'God, please let me win the lottery! Ah've lost my wee store, ma hoose and ah'm going to lose ma car as well.'

Lottery night again! Still no luck. Jock prays again.

'Ah've lost ma business, ma hoose and ma car. Ma bairns are starving. Ah dinnae often ask Ye for help and ah have always been a good servant to Ye. PLEASE just let me win the lottery this one time so ah can get back on ma feet!'

Suddenly there is a blinding flash as the heavens open and the voice of God Himself thunders, in a very Weegie accent, 'Gees a brek here, Eric. Meet Me halfway, ya miserable, moanin' Edinbugger gobshite. Buy a ticket!'

* * * * *

A historian decided to write a book about famous churches around the world. For his first chapter he decided to write about famous Scottish cathedrals and churches. He started in Hawick thinking that he would work his way northwards. On his first day he was inside a church taking photographs when he noticed a golden telephone mounted on the wall with a sign that read, '£10,000 per call.'

The historian, intrigued, asked a minister who was strolling by what the telephone was used for. He replied that it was a direct line to heaven and that for £10,000 you could talk to God. The writer thanked him and went on his way.

Next stop was Peebles. There, at the local church he saw the same golden telephone with the same sign under it. He wondered if this was the same kind of telephone he saw in Hawick and he asked a passer-by what its purpose was. She told him that it was a direct line to heaven and that for £10,000 he could talk to God. 'Okay, thank you,' said the historian.

He then travelled all over the Borders and in every church he saw the same golden telephone with the same '£10,000 per call' sign under it.

With his first chapter going well, he went to St. Giles Cathedral in Edinburgh, and there was the

same golden telephone, '£10,000 per call.' His final call was to Glasgow Cathedral, but this time the sign read '10p per call.'

The historian was surprised so he asked the priest about the sign. 'I've travelled all over Scotland, and I've seen this same golden telephone in many cathedrals and churches. I'm told that it is a direct line to heaven, but in all the other cities the price was £10,000 per call. Why is it so cheap here?'

The priest smiled and answered, 'You're in Glasgow now, my son. From here it's a local call.'

An Edinburgh couple on their way to get married were tragically killed in a terrible crash. Upon presenting themselves to St Peter at the gates to heaven, they asked if they could get married, specifying that they would like the ceremony carried out by an Edinbugger priest. 'Give me some time,' said St Peter, 'and I'll check.'

They waited and waited. After several months, they asked again. 'I'm working on it,' said St Peter.

Months turned into years, then decades. Finally, after 30 years, St Peter came running to them. 'OK, now you can get married!'

However, after a few months of married life, the couple really were not happy. They sought out St Peter and asked if there were divorces in heaven.

'Are you serious? It took me 30 years to find an Edinburgh priest up here. I'll NEVER find a lawyer!'

A rich Edinbugger lawyer was near death. He was very grieved because he had worked so hard stealing people's money and he wanted to be able to take it with him to heaven. So he began to pray that he might be able to take some of his wealth with him.

A Weegie angel hears his plea and appears to him. 'Sorry, pal, but you can't take your dosh with you.' The man implores the angel to speak to God to see if He might bend the rules.

The man continues to pray that his wealth could follow him. The angel reappears and informs the man that God has decided to allow him to take one suitcase with him. Overjoyed, the man gathers his largest suitcase and fills it with pure gold bars and places it beside his bed.

Soon afterward the man dies and shows up at the gates of Heaven to greet St Peter. St Peter, who by sheer coincidence is also a Weegie, as is God, clocks the suitcase and says, 'Haud on a minute, you can't bring that in here.'

But, the man explains to St Peter that he has permission and asks him to verify his story with the Lord. Sure enough, St Peter checks and comes back saying, 'You're right. You are allowed one carry-on

bag, but I'm supposed to check its contents before letting it through.'

St. Peter opens the suitcase to inspect the worldly goods that the man found too precious to leave behind and says in surprise, 'You brought pavement?'

An evil atheist Edinbugger explorer in the deepest Amazon suddenly finds himself surrounded by a bloodthirsty group of natives. Upon surveying the situation, he says quietly to himself, 'Oh God, I'm fucked.'

There is a ray of light from heaven and a Weegie voice booms out, 'Naw, evil atheist, you are NOT fucked. Pick up that stone at your feet and bash in the head of the chief standing in front of you.'

So the explorer picks up the stone and proceeds to turn the chief's head to mince.

As he stands above the lifeless body, breathing heavily and surrounded by 100 natives with a look of shock on their faces, God's voice booms out again, 'Right pal, NOW you're fucked.'

28
WHAT'S IN A NAME?

An Edinbugger and his partner were driving their fuck-off sized Recreational Vehicle and were nearing Milngavie. Elister said to Cammie, 'It's pronounced Mulngabby or something like that.' Cammie demurred, a thing Edinburgh lawyers do a lot of.

Since they were hungry, they pulled into a place to get something to eat. At the counter, Elister said to the waitress, 'Cammie and I can't seem to be able to agree on how to pronounce this place. We're from Edinburgh. Will you tell me where we are and say it very slowly so that I can understand.'

The waitress looked at him and said: 'Buuurrrgerrr Kiiiinnnng.'

29

EDINBUGGER EDUCATION

DRAFT HIGHER GRADE MODERN MATHEMATICS PAPER 2006

HIGHLY CONFIDENTIAL

EDINBURGH REGION

Name ....
Rugby Club ....
Daddy's Company.........................

Question 1
Gavin has a spare ticket for Julian Clary at the Festival Fringe. But Benji and Adrian BOTH want to go with him. How long does he cry before giving them the tickets?

Question 2
Half of Peter's friends say that they went to school with Ewan McGregor. Another third say they were

Gordon Brown's flatmate at University. A sixth say that their dad played rugby with Tony Blair's dad and the rest say Sean Connery was their milkman. Only one is telling the truth, so how many friends does Peter have?

Question 3

Todd wants to be a lawyer, but is as thick as Edinburgh Castle. His daddy is a Freemason and a QC. How long before Todd becomes the Lord Advocate?

Question 4

Tamsin's Personal Trainer charges £250 a week, but has sex with her whenever she wants it. Jasmin's Life Coach charges £50 a week but has refused all sexual advances. Which one of the women weighs 19 stone?

Question 5

Princes Street is 2467 yards long. On average, there is someone begging for money every 195 yards. You walk at 3.1 miles an hour. How long will it take if you tell them all to sod off and work for a living?

30
HORSE'S ASK

The aspiring psychiatrists were attending their first class on emotional extremes. 'Just to establish some parameters,' said the professor to the student from Newton Mearns, 'What is the opposite of joy?'

'Sadness,' said the student.

'And the opposite of depression?' he asked of the young lady from Springburn.

'Elation,' said she.

'And you,' he said to the young man from Morningside, 'how about the opposite of woe?'

The Morningsider replied, 'I think that that would be giddy-up.'

31
OPPURCHANCITIES

There was a Weegie, an Edinbugger and Sharon Stone sitting together in a train going through the Highlands. Suddenly the train went through a tunnel and, as it was an old-style steam train, there were no lights in the carriages and it went completely dark. Then there was this kissing noise and the sound of a really loud slap. When the train came out of the tunnel, Sharon Stone and the Weegie were sitting as if nothing had happened and the Edinbugger had his hand against his face going, 'Oyah!'

The Edinbugger was thinking, 'The Weegie must have kissed Sharon Stone and she missed him and slapped me instead.'

Sharon Stone was thinking, 'The Edinbugger must have tried to kiss me and actually kissed the Weegie and got slapped for it.'

And the Weegie was thinking: 'This is magic. Ya dancer! The next time the train goes through a tunnel I'll make that kissing noise and slap that Edinbugger bam again.'

A Weegie and an Edinbugger are strolling along Portobello beach when they find a lamp. They clean it up and out pops a genie. 'I'll give you each one wish (it's Edinburgh) for anything you want,' says the genie.

The Edinbugger thinks then says. 'I believe in Edinburgh for the folk of Edinburgh. I'm sick and tired of all these Weegies coming to MY city, driving property values down, laughing, drinking and winning at football. I wish for a huge wall around Edinburgh to keep the Weegies out.'

POOF! (it is still Edinburgh) and it's done.

The Weegie has a think. 'Genie?' he says. 'Tell me about this wall.'

'Well,' says the genie, 'it's 500 feet high, a third of a mile thick, nothing can get in and nothing can get out.'

'OK,' says the Weegie: 'Fill it with water.'

A Weegie is walking along the beach in Millport when he discovers an old bottle. He takes the cork out of it and a genie appears.

The genie says, 'I'll grant you 3 wishes (it is a Weegie genie), but whatever you wish for, the Edinbuggers will receive double.'

'OK,' says Jimmy. 'My first wish is for a million pounds.'

The genie says, 'OK, but the Edinbuggers will receive two million.'

'Nae bother,' says the Weegie, 'I can live with that.'

'My second wish is that Rangers win the Scottish Cup.'

Again, the genie says, 'That's fine, but Hearts and Hibs will win the next two after that.' The Weegie shakes his head but agrees, 'OK, I can live with that.'

'What is your third wish?' asks the genie.

'Well,' said the Weegie slowly, 'I'd like to donate a kidney.'

32
WEEGIES' CASUAL ACCEPTANCE OF IMMIGRANTS

PART ONE: THE EARLY YEARS

Matt McGinn, of beloved memory, used to tell a tale of the day about forty years ago when he was walking past a primary school playground and he heard the words: 'Haw, Mohammed, you're het.'

33

WEEGIES' CASUAL ACCEPTANCE OF IMMIGRANTS

PART TWO: NOW

At a concert supported by the Scottish Refugee Council in Partick Burgh Halls in Glasgow there was a trio of Kurds from Iraq playing onstage, making joyful music, so joyful in fact that a few, and then a few more, and after a minute every Kurd in the hall, about twenty men, women and kids, were up dancing, giving it laldy big time. They were joined by some of the Glasgow-born present and they danced in a big circle in front of the stage. The guy in the seat next to me leaned over smiling and said: 'These fuckers are going to fit right in, aren't they.'

His mate said: 'Whit's the Kurdish for "Gaun yersel, big man"?' and then just shouted it in Glaswegian anyway. For those unversed in Weegie-speak this is a form of very serious approbation and encouragement.

One of the Glasgow-borns involved in the concert

was Steven Clark, who allowed me to use his song, 'Home Again', with its deathless lines about the difference between Glasgow and Edinburgh: 'One has a castle, the other a heart', in the first *Weegies vs Edinbuggers*.

He wrote a song to welcome our New Glaswegians and it was sung as the finale for the concert by everyone, including our New Glaswegians. I could hardly sing it for the lump in my throat. Here it is. The tune is Steven's own.

COMING HOME

Put a light in the window
Your brother's coming home
Set a meal on the table
Your brother's coming home
He'll be tired and weary
After all those years alone
He's coming home,
   your brother's coming home

Take the chain from your door
Your sister's coming home
Open wide your arms
Your sister's coming home
Don't leave her standing there

After all the pain she's known
She's coming home
     your sister's coming home

CHORUS
Coming home to a place they've never been
Coming home to a land they've never seen
Coming home to a family they have never known
     All Jock Tamson's bairns
       are coming home

He's been angry and afraid
Your father's coming home
He's been hounded and betrayed
Your father's coming home
And with every act of kindness
A seed of hope is sown
He's coming home
     your father's coming home

CHORUS

Bring her in from the cold
Your mother's coming home
Sit her down by the fire
Your mother's coming home

Make her warm, make her welcome
Before the chance is gone
She's coming home
    your mother's coming home

CHORUS

From Iraq and Zimbabwe
Your family's coming home
And from Turkey and Somalia
Your family's coming home
Seeking rest and refuge
They have never known
They're coming home
    your family's coming home

Coming home to a place they've never been
Coming home to a land they've never seen
Coming home to a family they have never known
    All Jock Tamson's bairns
    are coming home

Of course, in Edinburgh, they are John Thomson's Children, but one would like to think that there too they will find succour and refuge.

Or perhaps not.

34
A PLACE IN WEEGIE HISTORY

One of Glasgow's most famous welcomes was for Nelson Mandela, when he came to visit the first city in the world to name a street (or, more accurately, a Place) after him. It was Glasgow City Council's only successful joke, and as far as I know the only successful joke perpetrated by any city council, unless you count Edinburgh's parking policy.

The South African Consulate in Glasgow, back when South Africa was being run by a bunch of ruthless and racist fascists, was in Royal Exchange Square, but the council, God love them, changed the name of the Square to Nelson Mandela Place. Mr Mandela knew this, despite being in durance vile on Robben Island, and one of his first acts was to visit the city that had honoured him and simultaneously cocked a snook at the South African Government.

Ian Davison, another prodigiously talented Glasgow muso, wrote a song about Nelson's visit. I'm proud to say that I was there, the day Mandela danced in the Square. George Square, Glasgow's heart. We showed him ours and he showed us his.

The tune is Ian's own, and can be heard, with lots
of other seriously good stuff, on his CD, 'Right On
& Up Front', available from Clyde Tracks, 5 Dick
Street, Glasgow, G20 6JF.

MANDELA DANCED

Chorus
We'd sung about him for years
And there were speeches everywhere
But I'll never forget the cheers
When Mandela danced in the Square
We'd sung about him for years
And there were speeches everywhere
But I'll never forget the cheers
When Mandela danced in the Square

When Nelson came to Glasgow
After all his pain
Ten thousand people met him
And listened in the rain
The big umbrellas folded
And many heads were bare
But every face was shining
When Mandela danced in the Square

Chorus

When Nelson talked of duty
You could feel us hold our breath
And we were just a little uneasy
When Nelson talked of death
And when he talked of trouble
There was tension in the air
But we faced the future smiling
When Mandela danced in the Square

Chorus

When Nelson came to meet us
We made our feelings clear
We heard the songs and speeches
And clapped and stamped and cheered
We heard of peace and justice
And the freedom that we share
But we shook the City Chambers
When Mandela danced in the Square

Chorus

When Nelson came to Glasgow
To show us he was free
The greatest man in Africa

To give us his decrees
A giant with a suit and tie
And sober face and hair
The welcome seemed to move him
When Mandela danced in the Square

We'd sung about him for years
And there were speeches everywhere
But I'll never forget the cheers
When Mandela danced in the Square
We'd sung about him for years
And there were speeches everywhere
But I'll never forget the cheers
When Mandela danced in the Square

First published 2005
by Black & White Publishing Ltd
29 Ocean Drive, Edinburgh EH6 6JL

Reprinted 2005, 2008

ISBN 978 1 84502 072 9

Text © Ian Black 2005
Cover illustration © Bob Dewar 2005

British Library Cataloguing in Publication Data:
A catalogue record for this book is available
from the British Library.

Cover illustration by Bob Dewar

Printed and bound by Norhaven A/S

INTRODUCTION

Thanks to the tens of thousands of Weegies who bought the first edition of this collection of calumnies and insults about the Edinbuggers – these calumnies being intermixed with some harsh home truths, like Edinbuggers having all the qualities of a poker, except for its occasional warmth, and that the worst two things about any given Edinbugger being his (or her) face.

The people of the two cities have traditionally always regarded each other with the greatest possible loathing, mistrust and contempt. They are both absolutely right, which is one of the joys of living in Scotland.

I have lost count of the number of times that I have been standing in a pub in Edinburgh and addressed the person on my left or right side only to discover said person shrinking from me as if I was a stalker. Many times, when attempting to initiate a conversation in these circumstances, I have been asked, 'What is it you want?' I don't *want* anything, except maybe a little human contact, a bit of warmth, a sharing of opinions on any subject that you care to talk about.

Weegies do that contact thing without even thinking about it and by God do the Edinbuggers hate it. No introduction, no old school tie, no accent from a particular school is necessary. Incidentally, did you know that the public schools in Edinburgh all have their own accents and vocabularies, and that they can tell each other apart? How seriously snobbish is that?

And mean? Every Glaswegian knows why 50p pieces are the shape they are.

It is, of course, so that you can use a spanner to get them off an Edinbugger. And what's the difference between an Edinbugger and a coconut? You can get a drink out of a coconut.

Here is a further collection of jibes and diatribes about the tribe known as the Edinbuggers. Some are true. Some are not. The challenge is to tell them apart.

But it is just friendly jesting. Sure it is. Not.

1
ATTITUDES AND INSULTS

Scottish by birth, British by law, Glaswegian by the grace of God.

What are the two worst things about an Edinbugger? His (or her) face.

Mean-spirited? Official and unofficial response to Saint Bob Geldof's suggestion that a million people with money in their pockets should come to Edinburgh to protest poverty: 'You'll have had your march.'

There was an elegant lady shopping at Jenners when she noticed a less than well-dressed woman blatantly staring at her. She began to fear some complete disaster, like a dropped hem on her musquash coat or a scuff on her shoe, but suddenly the scruffy woman cried, 'Mrs Green from Corstorphine! It is you!' The lady's retort sums up the Edinbugger, as she said, 'Quaite the contrary.'

It was a great party. The Weegie brought the Buckfast. The Forfar loon brought a bridie. The Ayrshire man brought a haggis. The Edinbugger brought his brother.

An Edinbugger has all the qualities of a poker, except its occasional warmth.

What's the difference between a tightrope and an Edinbugger? A tightrope sometimes gives a little.

Edinbugger lifestyle tip
Increase the life of your carpets by rolling them up and keeping them in the loft.

'Is old Sandy a typical Edinbugger?'
  'Is he? He's saved all his toys for his second childhood.'

Edinbuggers never smash in a face. They merely refrain from asking it to dinner.

The man who invented slow motion movies got the idea while watching a Edinbugger reaching for the bill in a restaurant.

How do you know when an Edinbugger is about to say something intelligent?

When he starts his sentence with, 'A Weegie once told me . . .'

Edinbugger savings tip
Old telephone directories make ideal personal address books. Simply cross out the names and addresses of people you don't know.

My mum and dad are Weegies but they moved to Edinburgh when I was two and then sent me to Fettes, because they wanted me to sound like an arsehole.

The Edinbugger was dying. On his deathbed, he looked up and said, 'Is my wife here?'

His wife replies, 'Yes, dear, I'm here, next to you.'

The Edinbugger goes, 'Are my children here?'

'Yes, daddy, we are all here,' say the children.

The Edinbugger says, 'Are my other relatives also here?'

And they say, 'Yes, we are all here . . .'

The Edinbugger rears up in bed and says, 'Then why is the light on in the kitchen?'

A Edinbugger took a girl for a journey in a taxi. She was so beautiful he could hardly keep his eye on the meter.

Double glazing is doing great business in Pilton and saving folk a fortune. The kids can't hear the ice cream van when it comes round, so they take less heroin.

Three douce Morningsiders were in church one Sunday morning when the minister made a strong appeal for some very worthy cause, hoping that everyone in the congregation would give at least £10 or more. The three Edinbuggers became very nervous as the collection plate neared them, and then one of them fainted and the other two carried him out.

A Weegie was hopelessly lost in the hinterlands of Edinburgh and wandered about for days, ending up in Corstorphine. Finally he caught the eye of an inhabitant, which is not always easy in Corstorphine.

'Thank heaven I've met someone,' he cried. 'I've been lost for ages.'

'Is there a reward out for you?' asked the Edinbugger.

'No,' said the Weegie.

'Then you're still lost,' was the reply.

Did you hear about the last wish of the henpecked husband of a houseproud Edinbugger wife? He asked to have his ashes scattered on the carpet.

An Edinbugger was ill with measles. 'Send for my creditors,' he said. 'At last I can give them something.'

Did you hear about the Edinbugger burglars who were arrested after a smash and grab raid? They went back for the brick.

A Weegie was being tried for being drunk and disorderly. The judge asked him where he had bought the bottle of whisky.

'I didn't buy it, Your Honour,' said the Weegie. 'An Edinbugger gave it to me.'

'Fourteen days for perjury,' said the judge.

Glasgow High Court Judge: 'You are charged with throwing the Edinbugger out of the third floor window.'

Jimmy: 'It was my Weegie temper. I did it without thinking.'

Judge: 'Yes, I understand that, but don't you see how dangerous it might have been for anyone on the street below?'

'I have a very unusual Edinbugger watch to offer you. It never needs a battery or any winding. It has no hands, and no face of any kind.'

'But how can you tell the time?'

'That's easy. Ask anybody.'

What's the difference between an Edinbugger and a coconut?

You can get a drink out of a coconut.

'Did anybody drop a roll of notes with an elastic band around them?' asked the Weegie voice.

'Yes, I did,' said several no-longer-quite-so-languid voices in the Edinburgh bank queue.

'Well,' said the Weegie, 'I just found the elastic band.'

You can always tell an Edinbugger, but you can't tell him much.

Weegie tourist on Arthur's Seat: 'This seems like a very dangerous cliff. It's a wonder they don't put up a warning sign.'

Edinbugger: 'Yes, it is dangerous, but they kept a warning sign up for two years and no one fell over, so it was taken down.'

Said the Edinbugger to the boastful Weegie: 'Take away your SNO, your BBCSSO, your Scottish Ballet, your Citizens' Theatre, all that other national culture stuff, your Celtic, your Rangers, and what have you got?'

'Edinburgh,' replied the Weegie.

Why are 50p pieces the shape they are?

So you can use a spanner to get them off an Edinbugger.

How can you tell you are in an Edinburgh restaurant?

There's a fork in the sugar bowl.

The Edinbugger put a penny in a weighing machine. A card came out which said, 'You are a friendly spendthrift.'

It got his weight wrong too.

2
WEEGIE INSULTS
ABOUT DUMB EDINBUGGERS

He's got the full six-pack, but husnae the plastic hingmy to hold it all together.

A gross ignoramus: 144 times worse than an ordinary ignoramus.

He's an ignoranus – an ignorant arsehole.

He donated his brain to science before he was finished using it.

He fell out of his family tree.

The gates are shut, the lights are flashing, but the train isn't coming.

He has two brains – one is lost and the other is out looking for it.

3
NEIGHBOURS

A Weegie and an Edinbugger lived next door to each other in Morningside. The Weegie owned a hen and each morning would look in his garden and pick up one of his hen's eggs for breakfast. One day he looked out and saw that the hen had laid an egg in the Edinbugger's garden.

He was about to go next door when he saw the Edinbugger pick up the egg. The Weegie ran up to the Edinbugger and told him that the egg belonged to him because he owned the hen. The Edinbugger disagreed because the egg was laid on his property and, as we all know, they know about property. Sometimes they talk about something else, but not often and never for long.

Anyway, they argued for a while until finally the Weegie smiled in that frightening way that they have and said, 'In Glasgow we normally solve disputes by the following actions. I kick you in the groin and time how long it takes you to get back up, then you kick me in the groin and time how long it takes for me to get up. Whoever gets up quicker wins the egg.'

The Edinbugger agreed to this and so the Weegie found his heaviest pair of boots and put them on. He took a few steps back, then ran toward the Edinbugger and kicked him as hard as he could in the balls.

The Edinbugger fell to the ground clutching his testicles, howling in agony for thirty minutes. Eventually he stood up and said, 'Now it's my turn to kick you.'

At this, the Weegie said, 'Ach, you just keep the egg, pal.'

The neighbour above was in the garden filling in a hole when his Edinbugger neighbour peered over the fence. Interested in what the man was up to, he politely asked, 'What are you doing there?'

'My goldfish died,' replied the Weegie without looking up, 'and I've just buried him.'

The neighbour was very concerned. 'That's an awfully big hole for a goldfish, isn't it?'

The Weegie patted down the last heap of dirt then replied: 'That's because he's inside your fucking cat.'

In Morningside lived a rich cat who was a bit of a snob, though she did deign to chat on occasion with her neighbour, a midgie-raking tomcat from Glasgow. One day she announced that she was about to have an operation but she didn't mention what it was for.

Two weeks later, the Weegie cat saw her again and inquired as delicately as he could how she was feeling, then dared to ask what kind of operation she had had.

'Oh, I am quaite well now, thenk you,' the Edinbugger cat replied, stiffly. 'I had a hysterectomy.'

'For Goad's sake!' the other cat exclaimed in exasperation. 'Can ye no just call a spayed a spayed.'

4
ARCHITECTS

How many architects does it take to change a light bulb?

Architect's answer: Does it have to be a light bulb?

Edinburgh answer: Does it have to be an architect?

Glasgow answer: It's not those fuckers who built the Parliament, is it?

5
PATTER

Weegie to Edinbugger: 'Why is your beer like shagging in a canoe?'
Edinbugger: 'I don't know, why?'
Weegie: 'It's fucking close to water!'

The Weegie beggar in Waverley Station shambled over, holding out his filthy hand, and said: 'Gonny gie a poor old blind man a pound, pal.'

'But you can see out of one eye. I can see you doing it,' said the Edinbugger.

'Everybody's a fucking critic, but let's be fair,' said the Weegie. 'Gies 50p.'

A Weegie was recently flying to London. He decided to strike up a conversation with his seatmate.

'I've got a great Edinbugger joke. Would you like to hear it?'

'I should let you know first that I am actually from Edinburgh.'

'That's OK. I'll tell it really slowly.'

So I was getting into my car, and this Edinbugger says to me, 'Can you give me a lift?'

So I said, 'Aye, sure. You look great, the world's your oyster, go for it.'

6
PUB TALES

If you want to get served quickly in an Edinburgh pub, learn to be polite. In Polish.

The token Weegie woman is at the office night out in one of the few properly grungy bars left in Leith. She is very attractive and has had a few. She gestures alluringly to the barman, who comes over immediately. When he arrives, she seductively signals that he should bring his face closer to hers. When he does so, she begins to gently caress his full beard, one of those annoying square-ended ones affected by Edinbuggers, who think that it makes a difference.

'Are you the manager?' she asks, softly stroking his face with both hands.

'Actually, no,' the man replies.

'Can you get him for me? I need to speak to him,' she says, running her hands beyond his beard and into his hair.

'I'm afraid I can't,' breathes the bartender. 'Is there anything I can do?'

'Yes, there is. I need you to give him a message,'

she continues, slyly popping a couple of her fingers into his mouth and allowing him to suck them gently.

'What should I tell him?' the bartender manages to say.

'Please tell him,' she whispers, 'that there is no soap, toilet paper or towels in the ladies.'

A Weegie is sitting in a pub in the Royal Mile one night when three Edinbuggers walk in. The men sit down, look him over, and classify him as not dangerous. Do not do this. Ever. All Weegies are dangerous, even the ninety-year-old blind ones. In fact, especially the ninety-year-old blind ones. Who else but a Weegie would have a killer guide dog?

Anyway, they start to talk about how they can noise up the Weegie. The first man says, 'Watch this.' He gets up, walks over to the Weegie, and says, 'Eh, I hear your St. Mungo was a poof.'

The Weegie replies, 'Do you tell me that?'

The Edinbugger goes back to his seat perplexed, then his friend jumps up and says, 'Here, let me try that.'

So he goes over to the Weegie and says, 'Hey man, I hear your St. Mungo was a transvestite poof.'

The Weegie says, 'Is that so?'

So the gadgie, frustrated, goes and sits down with his friends. Then the third guy jumps up and says,

'I'll show you how it's done.'

So he walks over to the Weegie and says, 'Hey, I hear St. Mungo was from Edinburgh.'

And the Weegie replies, 'Aye, that's what your pals were sayin'.'

As Donald the Edinbugger and Jimmy the Weegie were coming out of the pub one afternoon, it started to rain very heavily.

'Do you think it will stop?' asked Donald.

'It always has,' answered Jimmy.

An Edinbugger, a sheep-shagger and a Weegie are in Rose Street sitting in a noisy, smoky pub full of people. The Edinbugger declares, 'The pubs in Edinburgh are the best. You can buy one drink and get a second one free!' All the Edinbuggers in the pub agree and gave it vociferous backing. One guy nearly murmured and another almost said, 'Mmm.'

The sheep-shagger says, 'That's quite a good tale, but in Aberdeen you can buy one drink and get another TWO for free.' The crowd is stunned at this outrageous lie into a silence so thick that the staff were cutting slices off it and making up sandwiches.

'Aye, right,' the Weegie says, deploying the famous Scottish double positive negative. 'Your pubs sound good, but they are not as great as the Doublet Bar in Glasgow. There, you can buy one pint, get another THREE for free, and then get taken upstairs for a shag.'

The Edinbugger says, 'Really? Did that happen to you?' and the Weegie replies,

'Naw, no tae me, but it happened to ma sister.'

A Weegie goes into a pub in Rose Street and says, 'Quick, gies a beer before the trouble starts!' The barman looks around the sleepy pub, shrugs and hands the man a pint. The Weegie sclaffs it immediately. 'Quick! Gies another beer before the trouble starts!' The barman looks at him oddly but pours him another pint. He again downs it in a wanny. 'Quick, another one before the trouble starts!' The barman draws him another beer, with a frown on his face, and hands it over reluctantly. Again, the Weegie drinks it fast. 'Quick, another beer before the trouble starts!'

The barman exasperatedly asks, 'Look, exactly what trouble are you talking about?'

The Weegie says, 'I'm skint!'

7
WE'VE GOT A SUBWAY AND YOU'VE NO

Another thing that Glasgow has got that Edinburgh hasn't, as well as a sense of humour, is a Subway. Various groups have evolved The Subway Pubway Crawl, during which you get off at all of the 15 stops and go into the nearest pub. It is not compulsory to sing while doing this, but a lot of people do. They even make up their own songs for the occasion. Here's one that someone sent me. I don't know the author's name but if he (it's got to be a he) contacts me then the usual fee (a pint of beer of your choice) will be payable.

> *Oh Danny Boy, the pipes*
> *and pubs are calling,*
> *From stop to stop*
> *Along this subway fair*
> *My beer is gone*
> *The head on this one's dying*
> *'Tis you, 'tis you*
> *Must go and get them in.*

We're on our way
St Enoch's Square to Bridge Street
And on and on
West Street unto Shields Road
At Kinning Park
We dodge The Grapes and Doctors
Oh Danny Boy, Oh Danny Boy
Please get them in.
Cessnock, Ibrox
And Govan all sell Special
We drink some more.
Partick and Kelvinhall
It's time for food
We have arrived at Hillhead
And on the bar
Please put a half for me
At Kelvinbridge
The escalator's dead above me
St George's Cross
A Vodka and Red Bull
A Special please
At Cowcaddens, if you don't mind
Oh Danny Boy, Buchanan Street
Please get them in.

8
A NEW WEEGIE VERSION OF THE TARTAN ARMY CLASSIC

Do, a beer, a Mexican beer.
Ray, a man who buys me beer.
Mi, I'd like to have a beer.
Fa, a long, long way for beer.
So, I think I'll have a beer.
La, la, la, la, la, la, beer!
Ti, no thanks, I'll have a beer.
And that brings us back to Do!

9
GOLF

It is now generally accepted that golf did not originate in Edinburgh. No Edinbugger would invent a game in which it was possible to lose a ball.

After the first hole, the Edinbugger turned to his Weegie opponent. 'How many did you take?' he asked.

'Eight,' replied the Weegie.

'I took seven, so that's my hole,' said the Edinbugger. After the second hole, the Edinbugger asked the same question. This time the Weegie shook his head.

'No way, pal,' he replied, 'it's my turn to ask first.'

An Edinbugger golf pro, after ten years of retirement, went back to the game. He'd found his ball.

10
FOOTBALL

A new green and white Oxo cube is about to be launched in the shops in Edinburgh to recognise the achievements of Hibs. It will be called 'laughing stock'.

What do you sing to a Hibee taking a bath?
Happy Birthday To You.

A 22-year old secretary from Glasgow was on holiday in Miami. However, as she walked along the beach eyeing the big-bosomed girls walking arm-in-arm with their boyfriends, she became distraught, for she had a rather insignificant bosom herself. Suddenly, she spied a murky old bottle that had washed up on the beach, and for want of alternative amusement, picked it up. Poof! (Yes, they have them in Miami.) Out comes a genie, complete with flowing oriental robes, and immediately offers to grant her any two of anything that she desired.

'Give me a pair of the biggest tits in the whole, wide world,' she moaned. Poof! Poof! (Yes, two of them.) Immediately there emerged, before her very eyes, Scott Brown and Derek Riordan.

A Weegie walked into a pub in Lothian Road with a wee scabby dug under his arm, just in time to hear the Saturday afternoon footie results on the telly.

'Celtic three, Hibs nil,' said the announcer, at which point the guy shouted:

'Yes, ya dancer,' and the dog shouted, 'Oh no!' and started bawling his head off.

More than astonished, the barman leaned over the counter and said, 'Eh, your dog just shouted "Oh no!" '

'I know,' said the dog's owner. 'He always does that when Hibs lose.'

'What does he do when they win?' asked the barman.

'I don't know,' said the Weegie, with an evil smile. 'I've only had him for a year and a half.'

The same guy an hour or so later was waxing nostalgic about a previous pet: 'My wee dug watched all the games. When Celtic won it jumped up and doon and clapped its wee paws. When we lost it used to do somersaults.'

'You're kiddin,' eh? How many somersaults?' asked the impressed barman.

The Sellik man replied: 'Depended how hard I kicked it.'

A man, out walking his dog in a Edinburgh street, came across an old bottle from which a genie appeared, offering the man a wish. (The usual way with bottles and genies in Edinburgh. In Glasgow you get three wishes.) Startled, the gadgie asks if his dog could win at Crufts National Dog Show. The genie looks at the flea-bitten, limping dog and replies, 'I'm not a miracle worker. Think of another wish.' The man then asks, 'Can you get Hibs to win the Scottish Cup?' The genie immediately says, 'Let me have another look at your dog.'

The Heart of Midlothian. As well as being a football team, this is some cobblestones in the centre of Edinburgh. They're heart shaped, and it's supposed to be at the heart of Midlothian – the district Edinburgh is in. So, typically unable to come up with something witty or apt, they called it The Heart of Midlothian. It's supposed to be good luck if you spit on it and means you will come back. Rome gets a lovely fountain full of coins, Edinburgh gets some stones covered in spit.

Apparently, if you lick someone else's spit up you never have to go back to Edinburgh. There is always a queue of Glaswegians. OK, I made this up. Don't try it.

In Glasgow, we don't have a special place to spit, people just do it wherever they like. And often.

11
CINDERELLA

Edinburgh quick thinking (and a true story)
At Halloween a teenager in one of the nicer parts of Edinburgh was reported by a curtain twitcher to be having sexual congress with a pumpkin in a front garden. Here's the policewoman's account of what happened when she approached the young man.

'He was holding the pumpkin against the wall and I just went up and said, "Excuse me, but you do realize that you are having sex with a pumpkin?" '

'He froze and was clearly very surprised that I was there and then looked me straight in the face and said, "A pumpkin? Christ . . . is it midnight already?"'

12
EDINBUGGERS AND SEX

An elderly man was walking through the French countryside, admiring the beautiful spring day, when over a hedgerow he spotted a young couple making love in a field. Getting over his initial shock, he said to himself: 'Ah, young love . . . ze spring time, ze air, ze flowers . . . C'est magnifique!' and continued to watch, remembering good times.

Suddenly he drew in a breath and said: 'Mais . . . Sacre bleu! Ze woman – she is dead!' and he hurried along as fast as he could to the town to tell Jean, the police chief. He came, out of breath, to the police station and shouted: 'Jean . . . Jean zere is zis man, zis woman . . . naked in farmer Gaston's field making love.'

The police chief smiled and said, 'Come, come, Henri. You are not so old; remember ze young love, ze spring time, ze air, ze flowers? Ah, l'amour! Zis is okay.'

'Mais non! You do not understand. Ze woman, she is dead!'

Hearing this, Jean leapt up from his seat, rushed

out of the station, jumped on his bike, pedalled down to the field, confirmed Henri's story, and pedalled all the way back non-stop to call the doctor.

'Pierre, Pierre . . . this is Jean, I was in Gaston's field; zere is a young couple naked 'aving sex.'

To which Pierre replied, 'Jean, I am a man of science. You must remember, it is spring, ze air, ze flowers, Ah, l'amour! Zis is very natural.'

Jean, still out of breath, grasped in reply, 'NON, you do not understand – ze woman, she is dead!'

Hearing this, Pierre exclaimed, 'Mon Dieu!' grabbed his black medicine bag, stuffed in his thermometer, stethoscope, and other tools, jumped in the car and drove like a madman down to Gaston's field. After carefully examining the participants he drove calmly back to Henri and Jean, who were waiting at the police station.

He got there, went inside, smiled patiently, and said, 'Ah, mes amis, do not worry. Ze woman, she is not dead, she is from Edinburgh.'

A young Edinbugger was all set up for his very first sexual experience, but his girlfriend says, 'Sorry Farquhar, not without a condom.' He is totally skint and walking disconsolately around, knowing better than to ask anyone in Edinburgh for money, when he eventually meets Old Angus, a very good friend of his father. Young Farquhar explains his problem and is told in return, 'Don't worry son, I can help you out.' He vanishes for a moment and returns with a condom.

Farquhar takes off and the night is beyond his wildest expectations. A week later, he meets Old Angus in the street and tells him about his experience.

'It was wonderful, Angus. Thanks to you, I had the best time I have ever had.'

'Just glad I could help out, son. Now where's the condom?' asked Old Angus.

Farquhar looks at him and replies, 'I threw it away.'

Old Angus, with a scowl on his face says, 'Ah, you are in trouble now, laddie. That condom belonged to the club.'

13
NUTTY STORIES

A Glaswegian in Edinburgh for the rugby goes into a restaurant and orders a carry-out. While he waits, he grabs a handful of peanuts from the bowl on the counter, and as he starts to chew he hears a voice say, 'That's a beautiful shirt, is that silk? Very nice choice!'

Wondering who made the comment, and mindful of all the advice he has had regarding Edinbuggers' sexual proclivities, he looks around and doesn't see anyone nearby who could be speaking to him. With a shrug, he pops a few more peanuts into his mouth. Next he hears the voice say, 'That is a lovely sporran, my mannie. Is it Italian leather? It looks great!'

A little worried, the man decides to move away and play the slot machine. As he puts a coin in the one-armed bandit he hears a harsh voice say, 'You ugly Weegie prick.' He looks around but there's still no-one there. A couple of seconds later the second voice says, 'Fuck off, you smelly Glasgow tosser!'

At this, the man called the bartender in the restaurant over. 'Haw, I must be goin' aff ma heid,' he told the bartender. 'I keep hearing these voices, one saying poofy things, and one noising me up, and there's not a soul in here but us. If you are a ventriloquist, pal, you are deid.'

'Eh, no,' answered the bartender. 'That's the peanuts . . . they're complimentary, but the bandit's out of order.'

An Edinbugger in his mid-forties goes looking for a job on a building site in the East End of Glasgow. On meeting the foreman, he enquires about any vacancies he may have.

'Aye, well, I've just had to let someone go, so I'm a man down. Do you have any experience?'

The man pauses and looks anxious before telling him of his work history.

'Well, ye see, I've been involved in major con-struction work all my life, but I was involved in an accident a couple of years ago and haven't worked since.'

'What happened?' the foreman enquired.

'Well, to cut a long story short, I was working with a large industrial saw when it slipped and . . . unfortunately, I castrated myself.'

'Oyah!' the foreman said, wincing at the thought and studiously avoiding jokes about Edinbuggers having no balls anyway. 'Right, you obviously have loads of experience otherwise, so come down tomorrow morning at nine and I'll get you started.'

'That's great,' said the man, 'but don't you and your crew start work at eight?'

The foreman nods and, with a very Weegie grin, says, 'Aye, but we just stand about scratching our balls for the first hour.'

One misty February Scottish morning an Edinbugger was driving on the M8 into Glasgow. As he was passing Easterhouse a massive red-haired guy stepped into the middle of the road. The man is at least six feet four and has the appearance of a walking wardrobe. He has a huge red beard and despite the wind, mist and near freezing temperatures, is wearing only his trackies and a baseball hat at a rakish angle, held to his forehead by sellotape.

At the roadside there also stands a young woman. She is absolutely beautiful – slim, shapely, fair complexion, golden-red hair . . . heartstopping. The driver stops and stares and his attention is only distracted from the lovely girl when the red thing opens the car door and drags him from his seat onto the road with a fist resembling a whole raw ham.

'Right, you, Jimmy,' he shouts. 'Ah want you to masturbate.'

'But . . .' stammers the driver.

'Do it now . . . or I'll bluddy kill ye!'

So the driver turns his back on the girl, drops his trousers and starts to masturbate. Thinking of the girl on the roadside this doesn't take him long.

'Right!' snarls the guy. 'Do it again!'

'But . . .' says the driver.

'Now!'

So the driver does it again.

'Right pal, do it again,' demands the apparition.

This goes on for nearly two hours. The hapless Edinbugger gets cramp in both arms, he has rubbed himself raw, his sight is failing (as promised for years by his priest) and despite the cold wind has collapsed in a sweating, gibbering heap on the ground, unable to stand.

'Do it again,' says the Weegie.

'I can't do it anymore – you'll just have to kill me,' whimpers the man.

The Weegie looks down at the pathetic soul slumped on the roadside. 'All right pal,' he says. 'NOW you can give ma daughter a lift to town.'

An Edinbugger and a Weegie were sitting next to each other on an aeroplane. The Edinbugger leans over to the Weegie and asks if he wants to play a game. The Weegie just wants to sleep so he politely declines, turns away and tries to sleep. The Edinbugger persists and explains that it's a really easy game. He explains: 'I ask a question and if you don't know the answer you pay me £5. Then you ask a question and if I don't know the answer I'll pay you £5.' Again the Weegie politely declines and tries to sleep.

The Edinbugger, now somewhat agitated, says, 'OK, if you don't know the answer you pay me £5 and if I don't know the answer I pay you £50!' That got the Weegie's attention, so he agrees to the game. The Edinbugger asks the first question:

'What's the distance from the earth to the moon?' The Weegie doesn't say a word and just hands the Edinbugger £5.

Now, it's the Weegie's turn. He asks the Edinbugger: 'What goes up a hill with three legs and comes down on four?' The Edinbugger looks at him with a puzzled look, takes out his laptop, looks through all his references and after about an hour wakes the Weegie and hands him £50. The Weegie politely takes the £50, turns away, and tries to return to sleep.

The Edinbugger, a little miffed, asks: 'Well, what's the answer to the question?' Without a word, the Weegie shrugs, reaches into his wallet, hands £5 to the Edinbugger, turns away, and returns to sleep.

A Weegie and an Edinbugger who were stopped by the police for being drunk and disorderly. It turned out that the first had been drinking battery acid and the second had been swallowing fireworks.

The Weegie was charged and the Edinbugger was let off. The desk sergeant got a rocket for not prosecuting him.

14
THE TELLY

There is a local version of Big Brother in Glasgow. It's called Barlinnie. In Edinburgh it's Fettes.

15
GLASGOW ETIQUETTE

A pupil told his registration teacher that he would not be in on Friday because he was going to his sister's wedding. When he returned the following Monday the teacher asked him how it had gone. He also remembered that the boy's father was dead and asked him if he had given the bride away. The latter replied, 'I could huv, but I kept ma mooth shut. Ah grass naebuddy.'

Real quote from a Glasgow polis
'Relax, the handcuffs are tight because they're new. They'll stretch after you've worn them for a while.'

In Edinburgh a true friend will pay the bail to get you out of jail. In Glasgow a true friend will be sitting beside you in jail saying, 'We fucked that up, eh?'

16
LITTLE DARLINGS

At Cherrylaurellaburnum Primary, in one of the naicer parts of Edinburgh, Miss Fotheringill is asking the good little boys and girls of first year what their fathers do, so that the headmistress can mark out the future prefects. 'My daddy is a judge, Miss Fotheringill,' says little Samantha, brushing back the royal blue bow which holds her mane of freshly-washed blonde locks.

'Very good, Samantha dear,' says Miss Fotheringill, placing a discreet tick beside little Samantha's name in her big black book before moving on to the desk of little Roland.

'My daddy's a consultant surgeon, Miss Fotheringill,' says little Roland, his big blue eyes filled with the innocence of freshly cut church lawns.

'That's very nice, Roland dear,' says Miss Fotheringill, marking little Roland down as a future head boy and moving on to the desk of little Jimmy, whose father was a Weegie bookie who won the lottery and whose mother is a poisoner. Miss Fotheringill does not know this, but the tattoos of swallows flitting across little

Jimmy's neck and up under his ear has already drawn her to the conclusion that little Jimmy is definitely not future officer material. Nevertheless, she asks the same question of him.

'Ma da's deid,' says little Jimmy.

'Oh dear,' says Miss Fotheringill, overcome with remorse for her unkind thoughts about the poor lad. 'And what did he do before he died, little James?'

'He grabbed his throat and went "Aaaarrrr-ggghhhh," Miss.'

17
DEAD EDINBUGGERS

There aren't enough of them

An Edinbugger went to live in Glasgow but unfortunately (kind of) he died. Two Weegies went around from house to house collecting money to give him a decent funeral.

'Excuse me,' they asked up one close, 'would you contribute even just 50 pence to bury an Edinburgh man?'

'Aye,' said the Weegie, 'here's £10 – bury twenty of them.'

An Edinbugger woke up one morning to find his wife cold and stiff beside him. And she was dead as well. He jumped from his bed and ran, horror-stricken, into the kitchen. 'Marisa,' he said breathlessly to the *au pair*.

'Si, si,' she cried. 'What is it? Que pasa?'

'Just one egg for breakfast this morning.'

The insurance man knocked lightly on the door of the Morningside semi-detached. The widower, his black suit contrasting with his pale white features, opened it very slowly. He ushered the insurance man into the living room, where two (very small) glasses of whisky were poured. They sat in silence until the insurance man dug into his briefcase and then in a very quiet voice said, 'Everything is in order, Mr. MacDonald. Here is our cheque for £500,000.'

MacDonald stared at the cheque, 'Five hundred thousand,' he muttered. 'Five hundred thousand pounds for a life of goodness, love, faith, devotion and charity. You know,' (and here he stopped to wipe away a tear) 'I'd gladly give half of this back to have Fiona alive today.'

A Weegie stopped before a grave in an Edinburgh cemetery, containing a tombstone declaring, 'Here lies an Edinburgh lawyer and an honest man.'

'And who would ever think,' he murmured, 'there would be room enough for two men in that one wee grave.'

18
WEEGIE ATTITUDES TO BOOZE

And God said: 'Let there be voddy!' And He saw that it was good and partook mightily. Then God said: 'Let there be light!' And then He said: 'Haud oan, haud oan – too much light.'

To some it is just a bottle of Buckie. To some Glaswegians it is an entire Social Work department.

The problem with Edinburgh people is that when they aren't drunk, they're sober.

Time is never wasted when you're wasted all the time.

Glasgow saying: '24 hours in a day, 24 bottles in a case. Coincidence?'

Life is a waste of time, time is a waste of life, so get wasted all of the time and have the time of your life.

Reality is an illusion that occurs due to lack of alcohol.

If I had all the money I've spent on booze . . . I'd spend it on booze.

Buckie is proof that God loves us and wants us to be happy.

The problem with Edinbuggers is that they always seem to be a few drinks behind.

Give me a woman who loves beer and I will conquer the world.

You're not drunk if you can lie on the floor without holding on.

You know you're drunk when you fall off the floor.

And, as Tom Waits so memorably said for most Weegies: 'I'd rather have a bottle in front of me than a frontal lobotomy.'

19
LOTHIAN'S FINEST

Chief Inspector McSwiggan arrived at one of Lothian's police stations for his first day in charge, and gathered the entire contingent together for a lecture on riot control and crowd dispersal.

'I'm sure you all realise that we could be faced with a long hot summer of riots over this new Public Order Order,' he said. 'So I've asked headquarters to send us twenty armoured Land Rovers, 500 plastic bullet guns and 100,000 baton rounds for crowd dispersal purposes.'

'Waste of time,' came a muttered voice from the back of the room.

'Stand up that man!' roared the Chief Inspector. 'What is your name, constable?'

'James MacDuff, sir. They call me Weegie Jimmy,' said the constable.

'So, MacDuff,' said the Chief Inspector, 'you think it's a waste of time sending for all this extra and very necessary equipment which could very well save the lives of you and your fellow officers in an emergency?'

'I do, sir.'

'Well, MacDuff. Let us imagine for a moment that you are standing alone in the middle of Princes Street, confronted by an angry crowd of 10,000 who are hurling petrol bombs, champagne bottles and the spare wheels of Volvos. How exactly would you go about dispersing this mob?'

'I would take off my hat, sir, and threaten to pass it round.'

A Weegie candidate for the Lothian police force was being verbally examined. 'If you were by yourself in a police car and were pursued by a desperate gang of criminals doing 60 mph along one of our very narrow Lothian roads, what would you do?'

The Weegie looked puzzled at the simplicity of the question, then replied, 'Seventy.'

20
IT'S THE ECCENT

A young Weegie woman was on her first Mediterranean cruise and was talking to a douce Edinbugger matron who somewhat snobbishly announced that she had been on many, concluding by saying in that whiny Morningside way, 'My Elister works for Cunard.' The Weegie looked at her and said: 'This might just be our first cruise, but ma man works fuckin' hard as well.'

21

FOR ALL OF THE SCOTS, INCLUDING EDINBUGGERS AND WEEGIES

40 degrees – Californians shiver uncontrollably.
People in Scotland sunbathe.

35 degrees – Italian cars won't start.
People in Scotland drive with the windows down.

20 degrees – Floridians wear coats, gloves, and hats.
People in Scotland throw on a T-shirt.

15 degrees – Californians begin to evacuate the state.
People in Scotland go swimming.

Zero degrees – New York landlords finally turn up the heat.
People in Scotland have the last barbeque before it gets cold.

10 degrees below zero – People in Miami cease to exist.
People in Scotland lick flagpoles.

20 degrees below zero – Californians fly away to Mexico.

People in Scotland throw on a light jacket.

80 degrees below zero – Polar bears begin to evacuate the Arctic.

Scottish Boy Scouts postpone winter survival classes until it gets cold enough.

100 degrees below zero – Santa Claus abandons the North Pole.

People in Scotland pull down their ear flaps.

173 degrees below zero – Ethyl alcohol freezes.

People in Scotland get frustrated when they can't thaw their bottles of Buckie.

297 degrees below zero – Microbial life start to disappear.

Scottish cows complain of farmers with cold hands.

460 degrees below zero – ALL atomic motion stops.

People in Scotland start saying, 'Chilly, you cauld an aw?'

500 degrees below zero – Hell freezes over.

Scottish people support England in World Cup.

22
A WORD TO THE WISE

A wee old Glesca keelie is wandering about Edinburgh city centre for ages looking for a friendly face and a place for a bite that doesn't take a mortgage to fund. He sees a young barman having a fag outside a pub and the young guy gives him the Glasgow nod, that upward tilt of the chin that is unique to the city, and asks, 'How's it gaun, auld yin?' Delighted, the old guy goes into the pub and is served by the young guy. The pensioner asks for a bowl of soup and smiles up at the young guy and says: 'And maybe a kind word as well, eh son?'

The young guy brings the soup and as he is turning away the old guy catches his sleeve and says, 'And the kind word?' The young Weegie leans over and whispers in his ear, 'Don't eat the soup.'

23
DAFT, BUT NOT STUPID

There was a Weegie living in Pilton who always hung around a supermarket owned by an Edinbugger. The owner, Tim, doesn't know what Jimmy's problem is, but the Pilton boys like to tease him. They say he is two bricks shy of a load, or two pickles short of a ploughman's lunch. To prove it, sometimes they offer Jimmy his choice between a pound and a fifty pence piece. He always takes the fifty pence, they say, because it's bigger. One day after Jimmy grabbed the fifty pence piece, Tim took him off to one side and said, 'Those boys are making you out to be a fool. They think you don't know the pound is worth more than the 50p. Are you grabbing the 50p because it's bigger, or what?' And Jimmy replied, 'Well, if ah took the £1, they'd stop doing it, wouldn't they?'

24
ACCIDENTS

A Weegie and an Edinbugger were travelling on a motorcycle through windy Glencoe. When it became too breezy for one of them, he stopped and put his overcoat on backward to keep the wind from ballooning it away from him. A few miles further down the glen, the motorcycle hit a tree, killing the driver and stunning the man with the reversed coat. Later, when the Superintendent visited the scene, he said to the policeman standing nearby: 'What happened?'

'Well,' the young policeman replied, 'one of them was dead when I got here, and by the time I got the head of the lad from Edinburgh straightened out, he was dead too.'

An Edinbugger lawyer opened the door of his BMW, when suddenly a car came along and hit the door, ripping it off completely. When the police arrived at the scene, the lawyer was complaining bitterly about the damage to his precious BMW.

'Officer, look what they've done to my Beeeeemer!' he whined.

'You lawyers are so materialistic, you make me sick,' retorted the polis. 'You're so worried about your stupid BMW, that you didn't even notice that your arm was ripped off!'

'Oh no!' replied the lawyer, finally noticing the bloody right shoulder where his arm once was. 'Where's my Rolex?'